Bible Studies Books 101 and 102

To the Glory of God

Insights into God's Letter He Wrote to Us

Whom shall He teach knowledge?
And whom shall he make understand doctrine?
Them that are weaned from the milk and drawn from the breast.
For precept must be upon precept, precept upon precept;
Line upon line, line upon line; here a little, there a little.
—Isaiah 28:9–10

Steven Sprague

ISBN 978-1-0980-6191-3 (paperback)
ISBN 978-1-0980-6193-7 (digital)

Copyright © 2020 by Steven Sprague

All rights reserved. No part of this publication may be reproduced, distributed, or transmitted in any form or by any means, including photocopying, recording, or other electronic or mechanical methods without the prior written permission of the publisher. For permission requests, solicit the publisher via the address below.

Christian Faith Publishing, Inc.
832 Park Avenue
Meadville, PA 16335
www.christianfaithpublishing.com

Printed in the United States of America

Contents

Acknowledgements..5
Resources 7

Bible Studies 101

Study 1	The Bible 11
Study 2	Books of the Bible 19
Study 3	Studying the Bible...............................24
Study 4	Rightly Dividing God's Word (An Exercise) 30
Study 5	Gaining Personal Access to Our Heavenly Father 35
Study 6	Once Saved, Always Saved (?)..........38
Study 7	God's Book of Life 43
Study 8	Overcoming Temptation 47
Study 9	Removing Daily Stress from Our Lives............53
Study 10	Families and Rearing Children God's Way........59
Study 11	Worshiping God through Song and Music......66
Study 12	The Wife of Noble Character 68
Study 13	Understanding Death 71
Study 14	Capital Punishment............................75

Bible Studies 102

Study 1	God's Law and Grace 81
Study 2	The Three Earth and Heaven Ages 87
Study 3	The Kenites—Children of Satan 102
Study 4	Religion...108
Study 5	The Rapture Theory versus God's Word, the Bible.............................115

Study 6	The Birth of Jesus Christ (and Christmas)	120
Study 7	Levitical Food Laws	133
Study 8	God's Elect	141
Study 9	Parable of the Fig Tree	146
Study 10	Angels: Part 1 (Spiritual Beings)	151
Study 11	Angels: Part 2 (The Fallen Angels)	161
Study 12	Signs of the End	171

Acknowledgements

Thank you, heavenly Father, for this opportunity to serve you. Thank you, Father, for opening my eyes to see and ears to hear that through these studies, others might come to understand the simplicity of your letter to us, the Bible; that your truths, your love, and your Son Jesus Christ are brought forward in our lives. Thank you, Father, for your covenant—your free gift of salvation for all who might come to believe upon your Son with repentant hearts, to know and love you.

Words cannot express the appreciation I have for my wife Trisha, friends John and Mary Lachat and Norm Boldt for their years of ongoing support and inspirations.

I am continually grateful for the untiring labors of the late Dr. Arnold Murray, Pastor Dennis Murray, the staff of Shepherd's Chapel, and the people of Christian Faith Publishing.

Resources

These studies are an overview of varying subjects from biblical scriptures. Much more detailed information is presented in God's Word than is outlined here in these selected studies. It is my hope that your study of the Bible will prove to be as revealing as it has been for me. My Bible used for these studies is the Companion Bible, King James, Authorized Version of 1611 (Kregel Publications, Grand Rapids, Michigan) in conjunction with the Strong's Exhaustive Concordance of the Bible (Thomas Nelson Publishers, Nashville, Tennessee), and the Green's Interlinear Bible of the Hebrew, Aramaic, and Greek text preserved from the Hebrew "Masoretic Text" and Greek "Textus Receptus" following the order of the English Bible (Hendrickson Publishers Marketing, LLC, Peabody, Massachusetts).

I invite you to contact me via email at; 'steven.sprague99@gmail.com' with your biblical questions.

Your brother in Christ,
Steven E. Sprague

BIBLE STUDIES 101

"And wisdom and knowledge shall be the stability of thy times, and strength of salvation: the fear of the Lord is his treasure" (Isaiah 33:6).

The Bible

To many, the Bible can be summed up as "a mere translation of a translation of an interpretation of an oral tradition" and therefore, a book with no credibility or connection to the original texts. This is a misunderstanding by Christians and non-Christians alike.

In fact, the origin of the Bible is the reliability of the manuscripts from which today's Bibles are translated. Remarkably, there is widespread evidence for absolute reliability.

Over fourteen thousand ancient manuscripts exist today from which today's Bible is translated, giving evidence to widespread reliability from the Middle East, Europe, and Mediterranean regions that dramatically agree with one another. In addition, these manuscripts agree with the "Septuagint" version of the Old Testament, the Greek translation from the Hebrew language during the third century BC.

The Dead Sea Scrolls, discovered in Israel during the 1940s and '50s, also provide phenomenal evidence for the reliability of the ancient transmitting of Jewish Scriptures (Old Testament) before the birth of Jesus.

Long before the invention of the printing press, Hebrew scribes in those days dedicated their lives to copying the scriptures and preserving the accuracy of the Holy Books. They were highly trained to meticulously observe and count every letter, word, and paragraph against master scrolls. A single error would require the immediate destruction of the entire text, requiring them to start over from the beginning.

Some examples of today's historic and scientific communities of widely accepted early manuscripts are "Aristotle," with only forty-nine manuscripts in existence which were written fourteen hundred years later (after the fact) and Julius Caesars' "The Gallic Wars," with only ten manuscripts remaining, the earliest one written dating a thousand years after the original autograph. In contrast, the manuscripts of the New Testament, with over five thousand three hundred known copies in the original Greek, eight hundred were copied before AD 1000. And some text dating to the second and third centuries AD with the time between the original autographs and the earliest existing copies is only a remarkable sixty years!

William Shakespeare's thirty-seven plays written circa AD 1600 have gaps in the surviving manuscripts, forcing scholars to fill-in the blanks. Homer's *Iliad*, the most renowned book of ancient Greece, has six hundred forty-three copies of manuscripts. In those copies, there are seven hundred sixty-four disputed lines of text as compared to only forty lines in all of the New Testament manuscripts (Norman L. Geisler and William E. Nix, in *A General Introduction to the Bible*, Moody, Chicago, revised and expanded 1986, page 357). This pales in comparison with the over five thousand three hundred copies of the New Testament that, together, assures us that nothing has been lost. In fact, all of the New Testament, except eleven verses, can be reconstructed from the writings of the early church fathers of the second and third centuries AD.

The origin of the Bible is God. It is an historical book backed up by archeology and a prophetic book that has lived up to all its prophecies so far. God's letter to humanity, the Bible, collected into sixty-six books, is written by forty divinely inspired writers over a period of sixteen hundred years (1490 BC–AD 100). Divine inspiration may be unrealistic to some. Powerfully, the Bible validates its divine authorship through fulfilled prophesies. An astonishing six hundred sixty-eight prophesies have been fulfilled, and none ever proven false. God decided to use prophecy as His primary test of divine authorship, and an honest study of biblical prophecy will compellingly show the supernatural origin of the Bible. Skeptics have to ask themselves, "Would the gambling industry even exist today if people could really tell the future?" No other Holy Book comes even close to the Bible in the amount of evidence supporting its credibility, authenticity, and divine authorship.

BIBLE STUDIES 101

Science is filled with biblical archaeology beginning with the Sumerian civilization of about 2500 BC, through sites and artifacts uncovered about this ancient Mesopotamian culture. An example is the "Sumerian King List" dating back to 2100 BC, dividing Sumerian kings into two categories—those reigning before the great flood and those reigning after the flood, which show the same phenomenal life span changes mentioned in the Bible. Ancient law and culture is also evidenced by great military civilizations of Mesopotamia and their impact throughout the region such as the written laws of Babylon, known as "The Code of Amraphel (Khammuraen)" referenced in Genesis 14:1 and elsewhere. The Israel stele, a stone slab over seven feet tall with carved hieroglyphic text dating back to 1230 BC, describes Egyptian military victories by Pharaoh Merneptah and includes the earliest reference to Israel outside of the Bible. The Moabite stone, describes the reign of Mesha, king of Moab, circa 850 BC. This Shishak relief depicts Egypt's victory over King Rehoboam in 925 BC when Solomon's temple in Judah was plundered. This exact event is mentioned in 1 Kings chapter 14 and 2 Chronicles chapter 12. These are but a few examples of today's sciences coinciding with ancient biblical civilizations, accounts of history, and facts.

Translations, such as the King James Version, are derived from the existing copies of ancient Hebrew manuscripts, the Hebrew Masoretic text (Old Testament) or "Masorah," and the Greek version of the Jewish Old Testament known as the "Septuagint" and the Greek "Textus Receptus" or the New Testament. The Bible is not translations of text translated from other interpretations.

The difference between todays Bible translations are merely related to how accurately translators interpret a word or sentence from the original language(s) of the text source, which is written in either old Hebrew, Aramaic (Chaldees), or the old Greek language, or a combination of these languages in some instances, into the desired new language. To further complicate the accuracy of some translations we have to understand that it may not have been taken from the original texts themselves and then into another language, but may have come from an already translated Latin, German, or English version writing, and from there into yet another language.

STUDY 1

Did the translator have the knowledge necessary to fully understand other important language factors at the time of the translation such as; figures of speech (an expression which intentionally deviates from the meanings of its words), idioms (an expression not readily understandably from the meaning of its parts), or colloquialisms (informal speech) used in a particular area of the ancient world at the time period in which the text was originally written. The "mechanics" of languages must be considered as well, such as the use of certain prepositions, nouns, proper nouns, adverbs, adjectives, verbs, etc., which invariably differ between languages of the world.

For example, the word *was*, as used in **Genesis 1:2**, "[A]nd the earth **was** without form, and void; and darkness **was** upon the face of the deep." When properly translated from the Hebrew manuscripts, the original Hebrew word *hayah* (pronounced haw-yaw) means "to exist," i.e., be, become, come to pass, or as used in verse 2, "became." When the revisers of the English translated the original Authorized King James 1611 Version Bible, which had the word in italics, they decided that all italicized words of the manuscripts (carried through the Latin Vulgate [AD 1534]) and Geneva Bible (AD 1560), which are plainly applied in the Hebrew but require additional words in the English, be printed in common type. They had now failed to distinguish the difference between the verb "to be" from the verb "to become," so the lessons conveyed by the Authorized Version of the King James Bible are lost. Clear as mud, right? In short, the word *was* does not exist in the Hebrew language. When properly translated, **Genesis 1:2** will read (in part) "[A]nd the earth **became** without form, and void; and darkness **came** upon the face of the deep." Now the verse takes on a whole new meaning, prompting the question (for example), "What was the earth before it became void?" To quickly answer this question prompting a future study, it now participates in the clarifications of the existence of the three earth and heaven ages brought to life in the Bible—the one that was, the one that is, and the one to come and why.

Fortunately today, because of the sciences of literature and the lifelong pursuits of scholarly men, we now have tools available to help us to properly divide the Word of God.

One example of such a tool is the *Strong's Exhaustive Concordance of the Bible* compiled by James Strong and a hundred other men over the course of thirty years. Because of this tool, we no longer have to be fluent in the Hebrew, Greek, or Chaldee languages of old. Each and every word of the Bible, each place where it is used in the Bible, and the meaning of each word are translated into English from the manuscripts original language. The work also includes a Hebrew/Chaldee dictionary and a Greek dictionary.

Another indispensable work is the Companion Bible. This King James 1611 Authorized Version has undergone few changes since its original translation process from the original manuscripts. It was revised from this original Old English version to a more easily read English language of 1886, the King James Version we are most familiar with today. During the last four hundred years, many biblical scholars such as Dr. Schofield, Dr. C.D. Ginsburg, E.W. Bulinger, Moffett, Wesley, and several others have devoted lifetimes accumulating a wealth of information concerning original text, translations, analogies, archaeology, and facts about the Bible including such things as the chronology and history of man during these times, resulting in volumes upon volumes of research. E.W. Bulinger, beginning in 1910 and over a period of many years, collected these information's as a compliment to the King James Bible, creating the Companion Bible, first printed in 1922. These collections of research notes and appendixes are not his or anyone's opinions, interpretations, thoughts, suggestions, beliefs, commentaries, or new or amended translations, but only known and relevant facts placed in the margin next to each verse of the King James Version, taking us back to the original text of the manuscripts. The human element is excluded as far as possible so that we may realize that the pervading object is not merely to enable us to interpret the Bible but to make the Bible the interpreter of God's Word and will to us. Rather than having to research endless volumes of documents—the Masorah, manuscripts, concordances, histories, etc.—very simply put, the Companion Bible has done this for us in a reference column of right-hand margins in association with each and every book, chapter, and verse of the Bible. It also includes one hundred ninety-eight extremely detailed appen-

STUDY 1

dixes with a warehouse of information to enlighten and strengthen our understanding. It is an incredible work bringing God's Word to life, whether you are a scholar or a beginner.

The *Smiths Bible Dictionary* and an old-fashioned *Webster's Word Dictionary* are also invaluable tools in understanding the people and places of the ancient world, word definitions, origins, meanings, and more.

The following list is a chronology of the approximate passing of time since the beginning of this earth age in relationship to the Bible.

10000 BC	The creation of this earth age
6000 BC	Man created (the sixth day creation)
4004 BC	Adam and Eve created (the eighth day creation)
2348 BC	Noah's flood
1490 BC	Hebrew manuscripts (the Law of Moses Old Testament)
410 BC	Masorah (copies of the Hebrew manuscripts)
300 BC	Septuagint (Greek translation of Old Testament)
AD 390	Greek Textus Receptus (Greek translation of New Testament)
AD 400	Great Latin Bible or Vulgate (St. Jerome)
AD 1382	English translation of Vulgate (Wycliffe Bible)
AD 1534	German Bible (Gutenberg Printing)
AD 1535	First printed English version of the Bible
AD 1560	Geneva Bible
AD 1572	Bishop's Bible
AD 1611	King James Authorized Version (1611 Olde English)
AD 1886	King James A.V. revised (Revised English)
AD 2016	130 years later with many versions of the Bible now in print

In the beginning was the Word, and the Word was with God, and the Word was God. (John 1:1)

And the Word was made flesh, and dwelt among us, and we behold His Glory, the Glory as of the Only Begotten of The Father; full of grace and truth. (John 1:14)

All scripture is given by inspiration of God, and is profitable for doctrine, for reproof, for correction, for instruction in righteousness. That the man of God may be perfect, thoroughly furnished unto all good works. (2 Timothy 3:16–17)

The prophet that hath a dream, let him tell a dream; and he that hath My Word, let him speak My Word faithfully. What is the chaff to the wheat? Saith the Lord. (Jeremiah 23:28)

Now I beseech you, brethen, mark them which cause divisions and offences contrary to the doctrine which ye have learned; and avoid them. For they that are such serve not our Lord Jesus Christ, but their own belly; and by good words and fair speeches deceive the hearts of the simple. (Romans 16:17–18)

For I testify unto every man that heareth the words of the prophecy of this Book. If any man shall add unto these things, God shall add unto him the plagues that are written in this Book. And if any man shall take away from the words of the Book of this prophecy, God shall take away his part out of the Book of Life,

STUDY 1

and out of the Holy City, and from the things which are written in this Book. (Revelation 20:18–19)

The leading churchmen and theologians of England were called together by King James I to create an English language translation Bible from the Bible(s) and manuscripts of the original languages available in that day. These original writers, having been aware of God's warning and of their responsibilities, were so concerned of possible errors that they devoted the first approximate fifteen pages of their work known as the King James Authorized Version Bible of 1611 with an apology. The summary of their apology is that with all due diligence, believed they had done their best yet remained humble enough to ask forgiveness of God and man for any possible errors latter discovered. If possible, one should take the time to obtain a copy and read it.

Books of the Bible

The sixty-six books of the Bible including both the Old and New Testaments may be divided into six general groups:

1. Books 1 through 5: the Law
2. Books 6 through 27: the History
3. Books 28 through 39: the Minor Prophets
4. Books 40 through 44: the Gospels (good news)
5. Books 45 through 65: the Epistles (letters)
6. Book 66: the Apocalypse (revealing of prophecy)

The Old Testament

Book of the Bible	Meaning	Hebrew	Period
The Law:			
1. Genesis	In the beginning	Bereshith	4000 BC
2. Exodus	Redemption	Veeleh Shemoth	1446 BC
3. Leviticus	Worship	Vayyikra	1445 BC
4. Numbers	In the wilderness	Bemidrar	1444 BC
5. Deuteronomy	The words	Hadde Barim	1406 BC

STUDY 2

The History:

6.	Joshua	Jesus God the Savior	Yahsua–Yehveh	1406 BC
7.	Judges	Rulers	Shophetim	1380 BC
8.	Ruth	Friend	Ruwth	1200 BC
9.	1 Samuel	Asked of God	Shemuel	1105 BC
10.	2 Samuel			1010 BC
11.	1 Kings	Kingdom united	Israel	970 BC
12.	2 Kings	Kingdom divided	Israel/Judah	848 BC
13.	1 Chronicles	Words of the day	Dibrei Hayyamim	1000 BC
14.	2Chronicles			970 BC
15.	Ezra	Help (from confusion)	Ezra	538 BC
16.	Nehemiah	Comforter of God	Yahveh	445 BC
17.	Esther	Hidden star	Estthur	479 BC
18.	Job	Persecuted	Lyyob	1665 BC
19.	Psalms	Songs to rejoice	Tehillim	1000 BC
20.	Proverbs	The rule	Mishlai	970 BC
21.	Ecclesiastes	The preacher	Koheleth	940 BC
22.	Song of Solomon	Song of songs	Shir Hashshirim	970 BC
23.	Isaiah	Salvation of God	Yahveh	740 BC
24.	Jeremiah	Jehoveh has appointed	Jeremiah	626 BC
25.	Lamentations	Alas, pain, grief, wailing	Eykah	586 BC

26. Ezekiel	El is strong	Yehezkel	484 BC
27. Daniel	God my judge	Daniel	605 BC

The Minor Prophets:

28. Hosea	Salvation	Hoshea	750 BC
29. Joel	God is God	Yahveh	835 BC
30. Amos	Burden	Maseth	760 BC
31. Obadiah	Servant of God	Yahveh	855 BC
32. Jonah	Warmth of a dove	Yownah	785 BC
33. Micah	Who is like God	Miykayah	740 BC
34. Nahum	The compassionate	Nacham	620 BC
35. Habakkuk	To embrace	Chabaq	605 BC
36. Zephaniah	Hidden of God	Tsaphan	635 BC
37. Haggai	Feast or festival	Chagag	520 BC
38. Zechariah	Remembered of God	Zkaryahuw	520 BC
39. Malachi	My messenger	Malakiy	440 BC

STUDY 2

The New Testament

Book of the Bible	Summation of General Theme	Period
The Four Gospels:		
40. Matthew	Jesus, the true king	6 BC
41. Mark	Jesus, the servant of all	AD 26
42. Luke	Jesus, the man of compassion	6 BC
43. John	Jesus, the Son of God	AD 26
44. Acts	The acts (works) of the apostles	AD 30
The Epistles (Letters):		
45. Romans	God's plan to save us	AD 57
46. 1 Corinthians	The problems of the church Corinth	AD 55
47. 2 Corinthians	Paul answers his accusers	AD 56
48. Galatians	Christianity as a reality, not "traditions"	AD 49
49. Ephesians	We are one in Christ	AD 60
50. Philippians	Serve others with joy	AD 61
51. Colossians	Jesus is above all things	AD 60
52. 1 Thessalonians	Encouragement for new Christians	AD 51
53. 2 Thessalonians	The return of Christ	AD 52

54.	1 Timothy	Advice to young preachers	AD 64
55.	2 Timothy	Encouragement to a soldier of Christ	AD 66
56.	Titus	Instructions for doing good	AD 64
57.	Philemon	A slave becomes a Christian	AD 60
58.	Hebrews	A better life through Christ	AD 66
59.	James	How to live as a Christian	AD 49
60.	1 Peter	Written to God's elect	AD 62
61.	2 Peter	Correcting false teachings	AD 67
62.	1 John	The love of God	AD 90
63.	2 John	Beware of false teachers	AD 90
64.	3 John	Love to those who walk in truth	AD 90
65.	Jude	Warning of evil men and false teachers	AD 65

The Apocalypse (To Reveal):

66.	Revelation	Revealing (*Apokalupsis*) of prophesy	AD 95

Studying the Bible

We search for the knowledge and understanding of God's truths and promises that He provides us through reading His letter written to us, the Bible. With this knowledge and understanding, we receive wisdom from our Father enabling us to experience His deep and never-ending "agape" love for us. We learn to enjoy our lives through His love and grace and learn to love others as He commands. We learn to love Him in return, which is all he asks from us, as any parent desires from their child. He instructs us on how to live our lives while here on this tumultuous, wicked earth without fear, anxiety, or sorrow by having faith in Him in all things. His Word explains the end times of this earth age and His expectations of us and our roles during this time as Christians. It's up to each of us to take the first step. After that, His blessings never end as long as we remain faithful to Him. "For God so loved the world He gave His only begotten Son, that who so ever believeth on Him shall not perish but have everlasting life" **(John 3:16)**.

We have to *read* the Bible in order to *learn* from it. "Study to show thyself approved unto God, a workman that needeth not to be ashamed, rightly dividing the Word of truth" **(2 Timothy 2:15)**.

We have to *study* the Bible to *understand*. "Consider what I say, and the Lord give thee understanding in all things" **(2 Timothy 2:7)**.

There are *no secrets* from our Father. "Behold, I have told you all things" **(Mark 13:23)**.

Think about what you read—who, what, where, when, and why. Determine the subject. What is the message or thought put forward? Decide if it is law, history, wisdom, or prophecy, etc. Is it about the good news (gospels) of Jesus and His teaching, living life as a Christian, salvation, God's explanation of the three heaven and earth ages, or revealing of the end times, etc.? Jesus loved to teach in parables, providing the understanding of unchanging truths withstanding the passing of time and generations, applicable to any age, often by illustrations surrounding farming practices as an example. God often communicates or exemplifies in metaphors, symbols, images, and figures of speech, requiring an understanding of the "symbology" of the day. For example, how did a man living in 450 BC describe a flying object verses how a man of today would (see **Ezekiel chapter 1**)?

What's next? Prayer. Pray to our Father, the Creator of all things, and ask that His Holy Spirit would guide, teach, and reveal His truths to us and to give us wisdom in understanding as we read.

What Bible do we use? I have always remembered the evangelist's Billy Graham's response to this question: "Any Bible is better than no Bible." When I first started my studies, I chose a Bible that was easy to read because it was written in the more modern English spoken today. There is an inherent danger in reading a liberal text, however, understanding that the more liberal or colloquial the text, the greater the risk of error in translations from the original Hebrew, Greek, or Chaldean/Aramaic languages. We have learned over the years that even the original version of the 1611 King James Bible, considered the most accurate of English language versions, contains some errors in translations from the time period or clarifications by today's known standards of the original Hebrew or Greek languages in which the manuscripts were written. And of course, many versions of today's so-called "Bibles" contain interjections of man's interpretations far beyond anything even close to God's Word in accordance with the original manuscripts.

The original 1611 King James version has undergone very few changes and those that have been made we would consider "tweaks" of learned corrections from the original manuscripts. I describe it as translations back to the manuscripts rather than reinterpreting the manuscripts themselves. Fortunately, over the last 450 years, biblical scholars like the revisers in 1886 of their Parallel Bible to the original 1611 King James version, Schofield, Dr. C.D. Ginsburg, E.W. Bullinger, Moffett, and others including great textual critics like Griesbach, Lachmann, Tischendorf, Tregelles, and Westcott have spent lifetimes narrowing these issues to the extent of what we have today in explanations of things like the text, translations, analogies, etc., to supplement the Word—*not* an actual change of the Word. Our Father gives us very strong warning in **Revelation 22:19**:

> **And if any man shall take away from the words of the book of this prophecy, God shall take away his part out of the book of life, and out of the holy city and from the things which are written in this book.**

Now, the gathering of these information has created a compliment to the 1611 King James Bible, known as the Companion Bible, first introduced and printed in 1922 with these notes and appendixes collected by E.W. Bullinger from his original six parts beginning in 1910. These collections of notes and appendixes are *not* his or anyone's opinions, interpretations, thoughts, suggestions, beliefs, commentaries, or new or amended translations but only known and relevant facts placed in the margin next to each verse of the King James version, taking us back to the original text of the manuscripts. The human element is excluded as far as possible so that we may realize that the pervading object is not merely to enable us to interpret the Bible but to make the Bible the interpreter of God's Word and will to us. Neither is the Companion Bible associated with the name of any man so that its usefulness is neither influenced nor limited by any such consideration. It is a tool of collective knowledge and understanding of biblical facts, truths, chronology, archaeology, customs, money, weights, and measures, Hebrew, Chaldean, and Greek language translations, meanings, and so much more. Rather than having to research endless volumes of documents, such as the Massorah, early manuscripts, concordances, histories, etc., very simply put, the Companion Bible has done this for us in a reference column of right-hand margins in association with each and every book, chapter, and verse of the Bible. The Companion Bible also includes a hundred ninety-eight extremely detailed appendixes with a warehouse of information to enlighten and strengthen understanding—an incredible work easily understood by the beginner as well as the scholar, bringing God's Word to life. I highly recommend it.

In addition to the Companion Bible, I have found the *Strong's Concordance* and the *Smith's Bible Dictionary*, as well as *Webster's Dictionary* incredibly indispensable and useful tools. I no longer "skip over" words I don't understand or names I'm unable to pronounce and am able to better understand the importance of the original meaning of a word left in its original language, as examples. I now take the time and extra effort to understand as I go. And yes, I do read associated books by various authors of assorted subject matter pertaining to events of the Bible; however, be careful not to accept one's conjecture, personal opinions, guesses, man's philosophy or sciences, Hollywood films, etc., as fact but *always* refer back to the Bible to double-check such things against God's Word, which always stands alone as absolute. I am learning that the more I have been able to understand of God's Word, the less interested I have become of other writings because they no longer mean very much. The Bible is *very* clear on the information our heavenly Father imparts to us. We don't "pick and choose" what we want to accept or believe from the Bible; if God says it, so it is. If we are to believe any of God's Word, we must believe it all. I have also learned that things which are important to understand are "given witness" throughout His Word—or in other words, repeated, found in more than one place.

> **For when for the time ye ought to be teachers, ye have need that one teach you again, which be the first principles of the oracles of God; and are become such as have need of milk and not of strong meat. For every one that useth milk is unskillful in the word of righteousness; for he is a babe. But strong meat belongeth to them that are of full age, even those who by reason of use have their senses exercised to discern both good and evil. (Hebrews 5:12–14)**

STUDY 3

I would suggest that one might begin in learning and understanding the message of good news proclaimed by our Savior, Jesus Christ, as brought forth in the New Testament Books of **Matthew**, **Mark, Luke,** and **John**. Next, I would suggest learning about the beginnings of all things from the Old Testament book of **Genesis**, the first book of the Bible. If we don't know and understand the beginning, we'll never understand the end. Third, I would move directly to the last book of the Bible and New Testament, **Revelation**, or "the revealing." The entire Bible constantly interacts between the Old and New Testaments, and you will be referring back and forth often, thus "reading between the lines" and gaining a better, more in-depth understanding along the way. The Companion Bible easily walks you through this process in references and appendixes.

I regret with shame that I have wasted most of my life as a "babe" in God's Word. I am not nor will I ever be a biblical scholar or linguist, but I will live the rest of my life striving for "strong meat" in search of understanding in exercising my senses to "discern both good and evil." In this last generation of the end times, it is imperative that we read and understand God's letter to us so that we are not deceived, as Jesus warns in **Mark 13:5–6,**

> **Take heed, lest any man deceive you. For many will come in My name [teacher's, preacher's, priest's, rabbi's, etc.] saying I am Christ [a Christ-man or Christian], and shall deceive many.**

Why? Because few have ever taken the time to actually read to understand God's Word ourselves and have accepted or relied on man's word as may be taught by seminaries and the pulpits of today as "truths" without checking for ourselves exactly what God's letter to us, the Bible, states. Likewise, when choosing a church, we need to ensure the Bible and only the Bible is taught from the pulpit by a teacher who knows God's Word, chapter by chapter, verse by verse—nothing added, nothing removed. Not for our comfort or good feelings, man's traditions, or personal desires but only God's truths and facts, allowing the Bible to speak for itself, nonapologetic, and letting "the chips fall where they may." "Beloved, believe not every spirit, but try the spirits, whether they are of God; because many false prophets are gone out into the world" **(1 John 4:1)**. Read the entire **second epistle of John** concerning the same.

When we all stand before God in judgement, we will be alone before Him. The preacher, teacher, pastor, priest, rabbi nor anyone else will be standing with us coaching us. We have no excuses such as "Well, I didn't know" or "No one told me that!" God will surely ask why we didn't read the letter He wrote to us. "Behold, I have told you all things." What will we say? What can we say?

Eternity awaits us all, one way or the other. God has given us each free will to choose good, God's truths and love or evil, worshiping Satan's lies. Learn to discern the difference and how to return your love to our heavenly Father. We are all at different levels of understanding but all start with "milk." We must each work up to "strong meat" to gain "full age." Don't waste any more of your life. Start today, "for many will be deceived."

Rightly Dividing God's Word (An Exercise)

"Study to show thyself approved unto God, a workman that needeth not to be ashamed, rightly dividing the Word of Truth" **(2 Timothy 2:15)**.

To rightly divide the Bible is to correctly impart or reveal with accuracy biblical scriptures so that we can comprehend and appreciate God's message of truth with meaning and understanding.

Before proceeding, there are a few basic elements of English grammar that must be understood in order to increase our level of comprehension from reading.

It is imperative that we determine the "subject" of a text and the "object" of that subject as defined below:

1. *Subject.* A noun (person, place, or thing), or noun phrase (idiom or catchphrase) functioning as one of the main components of a clause (sentence) being the element about which the rest of the clause is predicated (based).
2. *Object.* Entity (thing) that is acted upon by the subject.

Using the following sentence as an illustration, "Tom studies grammar," "Tom" is the *subject* and "grammar" is the *object*.

The following words are often misused and misunderstood and need defined clarification to help keep our process simple.

Idioms. An expression peculiar to a language not readily understandable from the meaning of its parts, such as "to put up with," meaning to tolerate or endure: the language or dialect of a region or people.

Symbol. Something chosen to represent something else; an object used to typify abstract ideas, a quality, etc.: "The oak is a symbol of strength."

Translate. To express in another language, change into another language, or to explain in other words. Interpret.

Interpret. To judge in a personal way, to give the meaning of; explain or construe. To restate orally in one language what is said in another.

The New Testament manuscripts of the Bible were originally written in the Greek and Aramaic languages of the day (AD circa 60) and the Old Testament manuscripts were written in an Old Hebrew language common at the time (circa 1490 BC). The English translation Bible nearest to the one used today was first "*translated*" ("from one language to another") into the Old English language with the King James Version Bible of 1611. In this study, we "*translate*" ("explain in other words") from the more modern English of the Authorized Version King James Version Bible (circa 1886), extracting through the use of the *Strong's Concordance of the* Bible the earliest word meaning for clarity and understanding intended of these original languages. No attempt is made to "*interpret*" ("judge in a personal way or construe") God's Word as it is written.

Our research example is taken from the book of **Acts** written by Luke, recording various ministries of the apostles following the ascension of Jesus Christ. Peter's instructions are presented by God through "*symbolic*" (an object used to typify an abstract idea) dreams. In this instance, if the subject and object are not followed, the scripture is often misunderstood as an elimination of the Levitical food laws rather than God's actual intent, therefore, a good sample to work from.

Beginning in **Acts chapter 10**, the stage is being set for a meeting between Cornelius, a Roman centurion, a gentile of the Italian band with great fear (#5399: reverence) for the Lord and Peter, a Jew and apostle of Jesus Christ and the visions given these two men and their intended purpose.

STUDY 4

Cornelius's vision was pretty straightforward with the Lord telling him to go to Joppa and meet with Peter and "he will tell you what to do" **(Acts 10:3–6)**.

Peter's vision **(Acts 10:9–20)** consisted of a great vessel as a sheet with four corners let down from heaven, which contained all manner of four-footed beasts, wild beasts, creeping things, and fowl of the air. God told Peter to kill and eat, but Peter said he couldn't because (as a Jew) he had never eaten anything that is defined as common (#2839—defiled) or unclean. Peter is alluding to the foods which are not meant to be eaten by man as defined in the Levitical food laws **(Leviticus chapter 11)**.

A voice then said to Peter, "What God hath cleansed, that call not thou common" (Book of **Acts 10:15)**. This happened three times.

Emphasizing here that words have meaning, rereading the above verse, the voice said, "**What God hath cleansed** (#2511: purged, purified), don't call them common (#2840: unholy)." When we read again from **verse 12**, the vision "contained **all manner** of beast, creeping things, and fowl of the air." This means all types of animals, including both clean (healthy, purified to eat) and unclean (defiled, scavengers, unhealthy to eat).

The two men meet **(Acts 10:24–27)**, and Peter says, "God hath shewed me that I should not call any man common or unclean" **(Acts 10:28)**. Then Cornelius tells Peter of his vision, and Peter, recognizing him as a believer, stated,

> **Of a truth I perceive that God is no respector [#4381, one exhibiting partiality] of persons: But in every nation [#1484, race, non-Jewish] he that feareth [revere] Him and worketh righteousness is accepted with Him"** (Acts 10:34–35).

Peter, now realizing what God's mission for him was, went on to preach the gospel of Jesus Christ to the many gentiles that were there, and many were saved. Later, Peter told of this experience to his fellow apostles on his return to Judea **(Acts 11:1–18)**, and all the Apostles agreed; "Then hath God also to the Gentiles granted repentance unto life" **(Acts 11:18).**

God had painted a figurative picture for Peter that he and the other apostles would understand in utilizing the food laws to describe that which is "clean" against that which is "unclean" in His example. With this "symbolism," God did not state nor intend to change, rescind, or to make null and void the health laws of **Leviticus chapter 11.**

In **Acts 10:15,** Peter hears a voice stating, "What God hath **cleansed**, that call thou not common [unclean]." The "*idiom*" is that if God, through His mercy, has "cleansed" someone, referring to the act of forgiving a person of their sins, He has cleansed them regardless of who they are or were before their repentance and faith in Christ. All who believe, upon repentance, are accepted as His children, sharing in eternal life as His free gift to us. All mankind is equal in His sight ("no respecter of person") and have fallen short of the glory of God without His cleansing through the blood of His Son, Jesus Christ. It has nothing to do with the Levitical food laws but rather with the salvation availed to all mankind, Jew and Gentile alike; "that whosoever [anybody] believeth [have faith] in Him [Jesus] shall not perish but have everlasting life" **(John 3:16)**. Salvation would always include the Gentile as prophesied in the Old Testament including **Isaiah 49:6** and **Amos 9:11–12.**

The subject of **Acts chapter 10** consists of Peter (the noun) and "What God hath cleansed, that call not thou common" (the noun phrase). Peter's preaching, which is to include the Gentile population of the world, functions as one of the main components of a clause being the element above which the rest of the clause is predicated.

The object or the entity that is acted upon by the subject above is God's plan of salvation, opened to all mankind who believe upon His Son Jesus Christ and repent of their sins.

By following our *"subject"* and *"object"* established in our study example can one determine that these scriptures have nothing to do with making null and void God's food laws. To do so would require one to *interpret* ("to judge, construe, or explain in a personal way") that which is otherwise clearly written in the Bible, with an assailing repetition found in both the Old and New Testaments when rightly dividing God's Word.

Some may find it faster and more comfortable to utilize the proverbial *five Ws* as a memory tool with which to work through this process of comprehending Scripture as intended, as originally and divinely written by our Father, which bypasses all elements of time and varying languages of the world.

1. *Who.* Usually the main person(s), place, or thing (noun, noun phrase—subject).
2. *What.* The main idea presented—i.e., historical event, teaching, prophesy, etc. (object).
3. *Where.* Home, country, city, landmark, an area of wilderness, another dimension, etc.
4. *When.* Dispensation of time, period in history, future event, etc.
5. *Why.* Warning, explanation, instruction, reporting of facts, testimonial, promise, etc.

We have the tools to study with—the King James Authorized Version Bible in conjunction with *The Strong's Exhaustive Concordance of the Bible* (Thomas Nelson Publishers, ISBN 978-1-4185-4169-9), and a good dictionary, all to help us correctly reveal and impart with accuracy biblical scriptures. This is God's letter He wrote to us to lead, guide, and direct our daily lives to the fullest while here on Earth in these flesh bodies. With due diligence through prayer within His will, we can work toward God's approval and knowledge as a workman of His, spreading the gospel of His Son, Jesus Christ, and need not be ashamed of His simple truths that we might tell others of His wondrous love. He has told all things; we simply have to read of them with understanding.

Gaining Personal Access to Our Heavenly Father

The Israelites departed from Egypt after four hundred years of captivity lead by Moses. Throughout this forty-year period, Moses was in direct communications with our heavenly Father concerning the exodus. God's instructions were detailed, including things like the route of travel, position of each tribe during travel and encampments, to the specific duties of each tribe. Included of course were God's laws, statutes, judgements, and ordinances, such as the Ten Commandments, food laws, punishments for violations of His laws, and the ordinances surrounding worship, repentance, and blood sacrifices for the atonement (forgiveness) of sin.

The tribe of Levi had been chosen by God as the priesthood, which would perform the ordinances of worship required of God for His chosen people. This priesthood was first led by Moses's brother Aaron and then to be passed down from one Levite generation to the next.

For a deeper study, the complete details of these times is provided in the first five books of the Bible's Old Testament (**Genesis, Exodus, Leviticus, Numbers,** and **Deuteronomy**), collectively known as the Law of Moses, Book of Moses, Book of the Law, or Pentateuch.

One of the details of God's instructions in building the "mobile" temple of God during the exodus includes that of the veil dividing the tabernacle between "the holy place," a public area of ceremony by the priests from the "most holy place," a very private area containing "the ark of the testimony" **(Exodus 26:26–34)** in which only the high priest was allowed to enter once each year for the sin offering atonements **(Exodus 30:10, Hebrews 9:6–7)**. By the way, have you ever wondered what was inside of the "ark of the covenant?" Read **Hebrews 9:4**.

Without getting into an in-depth study of God's laws in the Old Testament through Moses and the transition to God's new covenant **(Malachi 3:1–4)** and laws under His grace through Jesus Christ in the New Testament, know that the blood ordinances of the Old Testament for the atonement of sins were replaced once and for all through the blood of Jesus Christ when He died on the cross for our sins **(Colossians 2:14)**. Greater detail is provided in **Hebrews chapter 9**.

In the moment of Jesus's death on the cross, the great veil of the temple separating the holy place from the holiest place of God Himself was torn from top to bottom **(Matthew 27:50–51)**. Through the blood of Jesus, we now have direct access into the holy of holy and unto the Father Himself and His household **(Ephesians 2:18–19)**. Because of Jesus and our faith in him **(Romans 5:2)**, we may know with confidence that we can enter boldly unto Him **(Ephesians 3:11–12)**.

Jesus became our High Priest that we can come boldly to the throne under His grace to obtain mercy in times of need **(Hebrews 4:14–16)**. If we confess our sins, He is faithful in forgiving us **(1 John 1:9)**. Once we confess our sins, He doesn't want to hear about them any more **(Ezekiel 18:21–22)**.

The priesthood of Jesus is unchangeable, and only He is able to make intercession on our behalf **(Hebrews 7:24–28)**. Under God's grace, Jesus, the Son of God is our High Priest forever **(Hebrews 7:28)** and our mediator **(Hebrews 8:6)**. Jesus is in the presence of God Himself on our behalf **(Hebrews 9:24)** and, by His blood, allows us to boldly enter into the holiest **(Hebrews 10:19)**.

Through prayer, we can communicate with our heavenly Father at any time seven days a week, twenty-four hours a day. We never have to be worried or be anxious about anything. We simply have to let our requests be known to God with thanksgiving **(Philippians 4:6)**. Sometimes we feel that God may not have answered our prayer, but He hears them when we come to Him humbly, with a repentant heart. He will always answer in accordance with His Will and not ours **(1 John 5:14–15)**. Sometimes we don't even know what to pray for, but God's Holy Spirit does and intercedes on our behalf **(Romans 8:26–27)**. We must be patient, as He always knows what's best for us. Likewise, with severe warning, we must never blame God for the evil in the world as he knows no evil **(Jeremiah 23:38–40)**. Man brought evil into the world, not God **(Genesis 3:6)**.

Jesus teaches us how to pray to our Father in **Matthew 6:1–15**. God knows each of our hearts and minds, but He wants to hear from us personally. He loves us. We are His children. He wants us to talk with Him about anything and everything the same as any earthly father wants to hear from his children. Our heavenly Father will never leave or abandon us **(Hebrews 13:5)**.

Once Saved, Always Saved (?)

God's prophecy of a new covenant with man is given to us in **Jeremiah 31:31–34** and elsewhere in the Old Testament, transitioning the Law of Moses to the new covenant of Jesus Christ **(Malachi 3:1–4)**, blotting out the blood ordinances of the law **(Colossians 2:11–14)**. **Hebrews chapter 9** details Christ becoming our sanctuary and sacrifice of blood and why:

> **So Christ was once offered to bear the sins of many; and unto them that look for him shall he appear the second time without sin, unto salvation. (Hebrews 9:28)**

> **Whosoever committeth sin transgresseth also the law; for sin is the transgression of the law. (1 John 3:4)**

God established His new covenant (promise) with man placing His laws into our hearts and minds. He will no longer remember our past sins once He has forgiven them (paraphrased from **Hebrews 10:16–18**).

> **If we confess our sins, he is faithful in forgiving us. (1 John 1:9)**

> **For the wages of sin is death, but the gift of God is eternal life through Jesus Christ our Lord. (Romans 6:23)**
>
> **If we confess of the Lord Jesus Christ and believe God raised Him from the dead, thou shalt be saved. (Romans 10:9–10)**

Once one understands what Jesus has done and why on our behalf and accepts God's free gift of eternal salvation by faith in believing in His Son, our salvation becomes a sealed covenant (contract, promise, pledge) between each of us and our Father.

> **[In] whom ye also trusted, after that ye heard the Word of truth, the gospel of your salvation; in whom also after that ye believed, ye were sealed with that Holy Spirit of promise. (Ephesians 1:13)**
>
> **God is patient, not willing any should perish, but that all should come to repentance. (2 Peter 3:9)**

Repentance is the Greek word *metanoia* (word 3341 in the *Strong's Concordance*) and means "compunction for guilt, reversal, to think differently afterward, reconsider, transform, to change." So repentance not only means to recognize by our guilt a wrong doing (sin) but also requires us to reconsider, think differently of our wrong doing (sin), transform or reverse our thinking so that we transform ourselves in complete change.

By *confessing our sins* to Our Father, *believing in the name of His Son Jesus Christ and His resurrection*, and asking of our Father with a *repentant heart* for his forgiveness, He will forgive us and remove them from our name in the Book of Life by the blood of Jesus Christ and give us eternal life.

> **If we say that we have no sin, we deceive ourselves, and the truth is not in us. (1 John 1:8)**

> **If we say that we have not sinned, we make Him [God] a liar, and His word is not in us. (1 John 1:10)**

In **Romans 3:19–22,** God tells us that all of mankind is under His law, that because of the deeds of man, He had to create the law, therefore no man is justified (guiltless, vindicated) in His sight. **"For all have sinned, and come short of the glory of God" (Romans 3:23).**

However,

> **Being justified [vindicated] freely by His [God's] grace [good will and love] through the redemption [payment] that is in Christ Jesus whom God hath set forth to be a propitiation [atonement] through faith in His blood, to declare His righteousness for the remission [forgiveness] of sins that are past through the forbearance [tolerance] of God. To declare, I say, at this time His righteousness; that He might be just and the justifier of him which believeth in Jesus. (Romans 3:24–26)**

Clearly, God is telling us that His forgiveness of our *past* sins is granted to us by His love and through the atonement of the blood of His Son Jesus Christ to those that believe in Jesus. Who are the believers in Jesus Christ? Christians. Very importantly, note that God's forgiveness is for our *past* sins as Christians and *does not include future* sins which we are liable to commit.

The only difference between nonbelievers and believers (Christians) is that we may be forgiven of our sins by His grace when we approach our Father with repentant hearts and ask for His forgiveness. As believers, we testify that Jesus Christ is His Son and that He died for our sins. We have accepted Jesus as our Savior by faith. We are not forgiven of our sins nor do we receive God's eternal salvation by our works or good deeds. "For by grace are ye saved through faith; and that not of yourselves; it is the gift of God; not of works, lest any man should boast" **(Ephesians, 2:8–9)**.

When we fall short of the glory of God and sin or fail as Christians—and we will because of our sinful nature and the world of sin wherein we live—we need only to ask our Father for His forgiveness of that sin for which He is faithful to provide as His heirs, remembering of course that He knows our hearts and whether or not we are trying to con Him.

"For if we sin willfully after that we have received the knowledge of the truth, there remaineth no more sacrifice for sins" **(Hebrews 10:26)**. Yes, we can fall far enough away from God that without sincere repentance, we may gamble away our very salvation.

Jesus is presented with a scenario while teaching to a crowd concerning sinners and the forgiveness of their sin and responds clearly, "I tell you nay, but except ye repent, ye shall all likewise perish" **(Luke 13:1–9)**. The Lord continues with the example of the collapse of the tower of Siloam and people were killed accidently and repeats, "I tell you nay, but except ye repent, ye shall all likewise perish" and proceeds to apply the same example a third time in parable.

Unless we repent of our sins, there is no salvation. God has given His promise, and He won't break it, but if we break our side of the agreement with Him by sinning, because of His love for us and the sacrifice of His Son for us, He will still give us the opportunity to receive forgiveness if we ask for it with a repentant heart. Otherwise the contract is broken by our own doing (not His) and void as a result of our continued sinning without repentance, and we will be judged accordingly.

> **For it is impossible for those who were once enlightened, and have tasted of the heavenly gift, and were made partakers of the Holy Ghost, and have tasted the good word of God, and the powers of the world to come, if they shall fall away, to renew them again unto repentance; seeing they crucify to themselves the Son of God afresh, and put Him to an open shame. (Hebrews 6:4–6)**

God doesn't save us over and over again as that would be an insult to the sacrifice of His Son—to say that it wasn't good enough somehow the first time. We are saved once by faith with a repentant heart for our past sins. Not if, but when, we slip up and sin after receiving Jesus Christ as our Savior, we can be forgiven, and in forgiveness, it will be erased from our name in the Book of Life. Our Father doesn't want to hear about it again, and to our blessing, His covenant with us remains intact and unbroken. As long as we faithfully uphold our end of God's covenant with Him, He will faithfully uphold His end. That's His promise.

"For God so loved the world that He gave His only Begotten Son, that whosoever believeth in Him should not perish, but have everlasting life" **(John 3:16)**.

God's Book of Life

Introduction

Our heavenly Father Himself introduces us to His "Book of Life" very early on in His Word (the Bible)—the very letter He wrote foretelling us of all things **(Mark 13:23)**. "Surely the Lord God will do nothing, but He revealeth His secret unto His servants the prophets" **(Amos 3:7)**. However, it is incumbent upon us to read the Bible as instructed, rightly dividing His Word **(2 Timothy 2:15)** that the Lord might give us understanding in all things **(2 Timothy 2:7)**.

When Moses returned from the mount where he had received the ten commandments from God, he found the Israelites committing idolatry and asked God to forgive them of their sins against Him and, if not, asked that he himself be blotted out of "Thy Book which Thou hast written" in exchange for their lives. God tells Moses, "Whoever hath sinned against Me, him will I blot out of My book," concluding with "when I visit I will visit their sin upon them" **(Exodus 32:7–34)**. This closing statement by God emphasizes the fact that we each answer individually for our sins, and there is a postponed judgement against those that have sinned against Him as recorded in His Book, which Our Father Himself has written—the Book of Life.

Definitions

The word *book* in Hebrew is "caphar" (#5612/5608) and means "to score with a mark, tally or record, to scribe, enumerate, recount, count, declare, or number." It also means "writing of a document, book, evidence, letter, register, and scroll." The Greek word is *biblus* or *biblion* (#976/975) meaning "a sheet or scroll of writing, book, a roll, or bill."

The word *life* in Hebrew is "chay" (#2416/2421), derived from several roots i.e., (#5315/7307) collectively establishing the meaning(s) "to live, living creature or thing, alive, revive, give, recover, restore, save life, be whole, mortality, breathing creature, soul, or spirit." The word *life* in the Greek language is "zoe" (#2222/2198 and 5594) meaning "life, to live, quick, spirit, and breath." In all of these manifestations, from the life of God down to the lowest vegetable, it is the opposite of death. It (life) also involves resurrected life and eternal life as gifted from our Father and so stated in **Romans 6:23**.

Salvation—Life Eternal

God's Book of Life is talked about throughout the Bible. For example, Job tells us, "[H]is Witness is in heaven and his record on high" **(Job 16:19)**, referring to the documented evidence of his life held by God in heaven. The prophet Daniel speaks of Satan's period of tribulation in which God's people (believers) "shall be delivered, every one that shall be found written in the book" **(Daniel 12:1)**. The Apostle Paul asks the church of Philippi to help the women and others who worked with him in preaching the gospel "whose names are in the Book of Life," identifying them as fellow Christians **(Philippians 4:3)**. Jesus tells the newly appointed seventy apostles not to rejoice because they have experienced power over the devils (evil spirits) but rather because their names are written in heaven **(Luke 10:17–20)**.

What does it take to have our names written in the Book of Life? By our heavenly Father's grace (love) for each of us, as His free gift to all his children, "whomsoever will" through faith are we saved from eternal death—not good works, money, or power but faith **(Ephesians 2:8–9)**. Even though we are all otherwise doomed to eternal death, we each have the power to change our fate by faith—faith in the Lord Jesus Christ. By believing in Him, we will not perish (eternal death) but will have eternal life **(John 3:16)**. Without faith, it is impossible to please God, faith that He is God **(Hebrews 11:6)**.

God's new covenant with man, through His grace and the blood sacrifice of His Son Jesus Christ who died for our sins, that when our sins are forgiven, there is no more offering required **(Hebrews 10:12–18)**. We must repent (ask forgiveness) for our sins. From our hearts, we must ask our heavenly Father to forgive us of our past sins **(Romans 3:22–26)**, for without the forgiveness of sin, there is no salvation **(Luke 13:3–5)**. Jesus makes this very clear when he states, "[E]xcept ye repent, ye shall all likewise perish"—twice spoken for emphasis **(Luke 13:1–5)**. Within this scripture, we see that accidents can happen in our lives at any time, therefore we must always be prepared. Prepared by avoiding sinful ways and on realization that we have sinned, we need to be quick to repent that we might reinstate ourselves in good standing before God.

When we have repented of our past sins, asking our heavenly Father to forgive us of them, God is faithful in forgiving us **(1 John 1:9)**. And on accepting Jesus Christ as our Lord and Savior by faith in Him as the Son of God that God raised Him from the dead, "thou shalt be saved" **(Romans 10:9–10)**. Once saved, we become a "new man," having rid ourselves of the "old man," the old ways of our sinful nature shown in **Colossians 3:1–10**, being renewed in the spirit of our minds **(Ephesians 4:22–24)**. As new creatures in Christ, God has reconciled (joined) us to Him through Jesus Christ **(2 Corinthians 5:17–18)**.

Once our heavenly Father has forgiven us of our sins, He doesn't want to hear about them anymore **(Jeremiah 31:34)**. "I, even I Am He that blotteth out thy transgressions for Mine Own sake and will not remember thy sins" **(Isaiah 43:25)**.

Declaration of Evidence

This is the record (declaration/evidence) that God has given to us—eternal life that our names are written in the Book of Life **(1 John 5:11–13)**.

> **For we must all appear before the judgement seat of Christ; that every one may receive the**

things [plural] done in his body, according to that he hath done, whether it be good or bad. (2 Corinthians 5:10)

From this scripture, we realize that God is keeping a record on each of us, including both the good (good works) and bad (unrepentant sin), and tallying rewards and/or retributions.

The only things we can take with us to heaven are our good works **(Revelation 14:13)**. As Christians, we are judged by our Father equally, without respect to persons, meaning who we were or what our positions may have been on earth mean nothing but by our good works alone **(1 Peter 1:14–17)**. Remember, judgement is also a time of determining earned rewards for those who love the Lord. Even our clothing worn in heaven is fine linen made from the righteous acts (actions and deeds achieved in favor of God) completed by each of us, His saints (holy or separated ones—Christians), during our time on earth **(Revelation 19:7–9)**.

"Repent ye therefore, and be converted, that your sins may be blotted out when the times of refreshing shall come from the presence of the Lord" **(Acts 3:19)**. Through repentance of our sins, we are rehabilitated, renewed, our records changed, our sins blotted out or wiped clean from our histories when God passes judgement. Those that overcome (conquer) the sins of the world will not be blotted out of the Book of Life **(Revelation 3:5)**.

At the great white throne judgement, we will be judged by God from the information contained in His Book of Life according to those things (plural), our works **(Revelation 20:11–13),** and those whose names are found not written in the Book of Life are cast into the lake of fire **(Revelation 20:14–15)**. Only those whose names are written in the Book of Life will enter into heaven **(Revelation 21:27)**.

Overcoming Temptation

Temptation. To induce, provide an inducement or act with which to persuade to action, one to do evil, or to sin.

"Every man [human] is tempted when he is drawn away of his own lust and enticed" **(James 1:14).** Even Jesus was tempted by Satan as we are shown in **Matthew 4:1–10**. However, Jesus was drawn away by the Holy Spirit (as Jesus knew no sin, i.e., lust) to provide an example as to Satan's cleverness in deceiving us and as a lesson teaching us how to defeat Satan in knowing what the Bible says to combat temptations.

The Bible tells us in **James 1:13**, "Let no man say when he is tempted, that he is tempted of God, for God cannot be tempted with evil, neither tempteth He any man."

Note the word *tempt* as used in **Genesis 22:1**—"And it came to pass after these things that God did tempt Abraham, and said unto him (Abraham), and he said, behold, here I am." The *tempt* found here (and elsewhere in the Bible) is not the same meaning. When properly translated from Hebrew, this *tempt* in English is "prove."

"For all that is in the world, the lust of the flesh [mankind], lust of the eyes [evil desires], and the pride [boastings] of life, is not of the Father, but is of the world" **(1 John 2:16)**.

To "lust" is to desire something passionately. A much more definitive explanation is found in **Galatians 5:19–21**:

> **Now the works of the flesh [mankind] are manifest which are these; adultery, fornication, uncleanness, lasciviousness. Idolatry, witchcraft, hatred, variance, emulations, wrath, strife, seditions, heresies. Envying's, murders,**

drunkenness, reveling, and such like, of which I tell you before, as I have also told you in time past, that they which do such things shall not inherit the Kingdom of God.

Temptation itself is not sin, but the fulfillment of the temptation is sin as explained in **James 1:15**. "Then when lust hath conceived, it bringeth forth sin; and sin, when it is finished, bringeth forth death."

Now that we understand what temptation is, let's see what God's Word teaches to enable us to overcome Satan's temptations and relentless pursuit to deceive us. In order to combat temptations and sin, we must know and understand the Bible, God's letter to us.

1. *We must protect ourselves:*

As outlined in **Ephesians 6:11–18**, we must "put on the whole armour of God" that He provides to protect us, "that we may stand against the wiles of the devil." Here we learn this fight isn't against "flesh and blood, but against principalities," supernatural "powers," "rulers of the darkness of this world," and "against spiritual wickedness in high places." And again, God emphasizes, "Take upon you the whole armour of God." We will need it to "withstand in the evil day, and having done all, to stand." We stand with "truth," "righteousness," being prepared with "the gospel of peace" (Jesus), and "above all, faith," which will enable us to "quench all the fiery darts of the wicked," along with "the helmet of salvation" and "the sword of the spirit, which is the Word of God." Last but not least, "prayer" and watching out for "all the saints (Christians)."

2. *We must stay on the right path:*

Don't follow the crowd. "Thy word is a lamp unto my feet, and a light unto my path. I have sworn, and I will perform it, that I will keep Thy righteous judgements" **(Psalms 119:105–106)**.

3. *Look for escape routes:*

Run from the situation, as demonstrated by Joseph (son of Israel) early in **Genesis 39:11–12**:

> **And it came to pass about this time, that Joseph went into the house to do his business; and there was none of the men of the house there within. And she [the masters' wife] caught him by his garment, saying, "Lie with me" and he left his garment in her hand, and fled, and got him out.**

There is no temptation that isn't common to all mankind. We are not the only one experiencing temptation. God will not allow us to be tempted beyond our ability to withstand and remove ourselves from the situation.

> **There hath no temptation taken you but such as is common to man; but God is faithful, Who will not suffer you to be tempted above that ye are able; but will with the temptation also make a way to escape that ye may be able to bear it. (1 Corinthians 10:13)**

> **Jesus can keep us from failing. (Jude 1:24)**

4. *Resist Satan, be alert, and fight back with God's help:*

Remember that God had created Lucifer, who at one time was an entity of the highest order in heaven before his disobedience to

God and subsequent downfall. As God created Satan, so does God have the power to (and will) destroy him.

> **Ye are of God, little children, and have overcome them; because greater is He that is in you, than he that is in the world. (1 John 4:4)**
>
> **Submit yourselves therefore to God. Resist the devil and he will flee from you. (James 4:7)**
>
> **Be sober, be vigilant; because your adversary the devil, as a roaring lion, walketh about, seeking whom he may devour. Whom resist steadfast in the faith, knowing that the same afflictions are accomplished to your brethren that are in the world. (1 Peter 5:8–9)**

God gives us power over all our enemies, including Satan, when ordered in Jesus's name. "And the seventy returned again with joy, saying, Lord, even the devils are subject unto us through Thy name" **(Luke 10:17)**. And Jesus replied, "Behold, I give unto you power to tread on serpents and scorpions, and over all the power of the enemy: and nothing shall by any means hurt you" **(Luke 10:19)**.

5. *Be a survivor:*

Put your efforts into matters of spiritual life rather than the physical aspects of life.

> **Confess your faults one to another, and pray one for another that ye may be healed. The effectual fervent prayer of a righteous man availeth much. (James 5:16)**

We intuitively know the difference between right and wrong in most cases, and in those instances where we are not sure, remember an old saying of man: "When in doubt, don't." As Christians, on those occasions when we realize that we have sinned, if we repent of our sins, we are forgiven. By God's grace (love), this is His gift to us as a result of Jesus's sacrifice of His blood when He was crucified on the cross on our behalf, for the forgiveness of sin.

> **This is the covenant that I [God speaking] will make with them [believers] after those days saith the Lord; I will put my laws into their hearts. And in their minds I will write them. And their sins and iniquities will I remember no more. Now where remission [forgiveness] of these is, there is no more offering for sin. (Hebrews 10:16–18)**

6. *The price of sin:*

    > **For all have sinned and come short of the Glory of God. (Romans 3:23)**

    > **But now being made free from sin, and become servants to God, ye have your fruit unto holiness, and the end, everlasting life. For the wages of sin is death; but the gift of God is eternal life through Jesus Christ our Lord. (Romans 6:22–23)**

    > **Be not deceived; God is not mocked; for whatsoever a man soweth, that shall he also reap. (Galatians 6:7)**

7. *The solution:*

    > **For God so loved the world that He gave His only begotten Son, that whosoever believeth in Him, should not perish, but have everlasting life. (John 3:16)**

> Wherefore, lay apart all filthiness and superfluity of naughtiness [abundance of evil desires], and receive with meekness the engrafted [implanted] Word, which is able to save your souls. (James 1:21)

8. *Therefore:*

> Blessed is the man that endureth temptation; for when he is tried, he shall receive the crown of life, which the Lord hath promised to them that love Him. (James 1:12)

> And besides this, giving all diligence, add to your faith virtue; and to virtue knowledge; and to knowledge temperance; and to temperance patience; and to patience Godliness; and to Godliness brotherly kindness; and to brotherly kindness charity. For if these things be in you and abound, they make you that ye shall neither be barren nor unfruitful in the knowledge of our lord Jesus Christ. (2 Peter 1:5–8)

> This I say then, walk in the Spirit, and ye shall not fulfil the lust of the flesh. (Galatians 5:16)

> But the fruit of the Spirit is love, joy, peace, longsuffering [patience], gentleness, goodness, faith, meekness, temperance: against such there is no law. And they that are Christ's have crucified the flesh with the affections and lusts. If we live in the Spirit, let us also walk in the Spirit. Let us not be desirous of vain glory, provoking one another, envying one another. (Galatians 5:22–26)

Removing Daily Stress from Our Lives

Our Father loves us and invites us (His children) to come to Him in all things. He allows us to talk directly with Him in prayer without the need for an intercessory anytime day or night, seven days a week **(Ephesians 2:18–19; 3:11–12)**. He has given us the Comforter, His Holy Spirit, to guide, direct, and teach us in all things **(John 14:26)** that we can enjoy to the fullest His blessings and His gift of eternal life through His Son Jesus **(John 3:16)**, both on earth and in heaven, together with Him for eternity.

Today, our daily existence includes ever-increasing requirements far beyond yesterday's demands of hunting and planting. Stress created within ourselves is a result of many factors including insufficient hours within the day to complete our goals, jobs, family, relationships, marriages, deaths, illnesses, divorces, unemployment, financial obligations, community responsibilities, rising prices, shrinking incomes, social engagements, rising crime rates, and more. Our entire environment has become an endless list of problems quickening an early demise for each of us. It's crazy! It's driving us crazy! Yet we keep piling more and more on ourselves!

For a sense of relief, many turn to alcohol, illegal and/or legal drugs, and worse. None of which is, nor has ever been, the permanent answer to any problem.

The Bible tells us that as the end of this earth age nears, there will be "times of trouble such as never was" **(Daniel 12:1; Mark 13:19)**, increasing man's level of stress and fears to the limits.

STUDY 9

There is an answer, only one answer. There is hope, only one hope. It is offered by our Father in heaven. He gives us guidance through His Word, providing wisdom, assuring hope, peace, and a perfect eternity through Jesus Christ. "And the peace of God, which passeth all understanding, shall keep your hearts and minds through Christ Jesus" (**Philippians 4:7**). In all troubles, God will provide you peace—a peace beyond human understanding, in our thoughts and hearts as a protective shield against all evil through Jesus Christ.

> **The righteous cry and The Lord heareth and delivereth them out of all their troubles. The Lord is nigh unto them that are of broken heart; and saveth such as be of a contrite spirit. Many are the afflictions of the righteous, but The Lord delivereth him out of them all. (Psalms 34:17–19)**

God hears the cries and requests of His children and will remove you from your troubles. He holds you in His arms when your heart is broken and understands all of your feelings and will save those that are truly and humbly sorry for their sins. He knows and understands that His children suffer many things here on earth as a result of sin in the world, yet He will take us out of them all.

"He knows what we have **need** of before we even ask" (**Matthew 6:8**). Keep in mind however, that most of us probably don't have a real *need* for that "Mercedes Benz."

> **Ask and it shall be given you; seek, and ye shall find; knock, and it shall be open unto you. (Matthew 7:7)**
>
> **And all things, whatsoever ye shall ask in prayer, believing, ye shall receive. (Matthew 21:22)**

We must be realistic here as well, remembering what Jesus said to the disciples as He was teaching them how to pray to our Father:

"Thy will [God's, not ours] be done in earth, as it is in heaven" **(Matthew 6:10)**. God is almighty, all-seeing, and all-knowing. Our Father cannot and will not be conned. He certainly knows our needs, and if what we pray for is not contrary to His will, He will provide in His time, not ours, what He knows is best for us, not what we think is best for ourselves.

Like any father, our heavenly Father knows of things that we have no thought of. For example, if a ten-year-old child came to you asking for a car of their own, because of your wisdom and knowledge of the imminent dangers resulting from such an act, you are likely to deny that child's request—at least for a time. However, you might be inclined to encourage them to begin working toward their goal themselves, perhaps offering them a job within the household. Our heavenly Father is no different. He always knows what's best for us.

"Let your conversation be without covetousness; and be content with such things as ye have; for He [God] hath said, I will never leave thee, nor forsake thee" **(Hebrews 13: 5)**. In other words, live your life in such a manner that you don't live for the love of money or "things." Be content and always thankful for what you do have. God promises He'll never leave you or abandon you, and remember, He knows what you have *need* for before you even ask!

Talk to Him, He is your Father. Ask Him for His help. "Be careful for nothing; but in everything by prayer and supplication with thanksgiving let your requests be made known unto God" **(Philippians 4:6)**. Don't worry about anything, but through prayer, make your needs known to our Father with a thankful heart.

"Cast thy burden upon The Lord and He shall sustain thee. He shall never suffer the righteous to be moved" **(Psalms 55:22)**. As our Father, God is telling you to turn your problems over to Him and He'll stand with you and give you strength. As a believer, when we ask for His help, He will not tolerate Satan's evilness to turn you away from Him.

"For I know the thoughts that I think toward you, saith The Lord, thoughts of peace, and not of evil, to give you an expected end" **(Jeremiah 29:11).** Our Father has only good wishes and peace for his children. He never wishes you any harm or evil and truly desires to fulfill your expectation in accordance to His will.

> **Humble yourselves therefore, under the mighty hand of God, that He may exalt you in due time. Casting all your care upon Him; for He careth for you. Be sober, be vigilant; because your adversary the devil, as a roaring lion, walketh about, seeking whom he may devour. (1 Peter 4:6–8)**

We need to remember who we are in relation to almighty God, being humble before Him as one of His children, and allow Him the opportunity to delight us, as a surprise, in His due time. Again, He asks that we turn all our burdens over to Him because He cares for us and wants to protect us. However, He still expects us to be watchful and knowledgeable of our surroundings, cognitive of our personal actions, and strive to be obedient to Him because Satan is lurking at every turn to snare us into his trap.

"Therefore I say unto you, take no thought for your life, what ye shall eat, or what ye shall drink; nor yet for your body what ye shall put on. Is not the life more than meat, and the body than raiment?" **(Matthew 6:25)**. Here, Jesus tells us not to worry about life, what you're going to eat or drink, or wear and asks us if our soul itself isn't more important than food or clothes?

"Behold the fowls of the air; for they sow not, neither do they reap, nor gather into barns; yet your heavenly Father feedeth them. Are ye not much better than they?" **(v. 26)**. Jesus points at the birds in the sky, reminding us that they don't plant or harvest or build their own shelters, yet our Father in heaven feeds them and takes care of them just fine. Don't you think that He cares much more for you, His child, than He does for the birds?

"Which of you by taking thought can add one cubit unto his stature?" **(v. 27)**. In other words, who among you can "think" or "meditate" their way into prolonging or adding one measurable moment to your life?

"And why take ye thought for raiment? Consider the lilies of the field, how they grow; they toil not, neither do they spin" **(v. 28)**. Jesus asks, why worry about what clothes you wear? Think about how lilies grow and how beautiful they are, yet they don't work for a living or manufacture their own clothing.

"And yet I say unto you, that even Solomon in all his glory was not arrayed like one of these" **(v. 29)**. Even King Solomon, with all his wealth and riches, wasn't dressed as beautifully as a simple lily.

"Wherefore, if God so clothe the grass of the field, which today is, and tomorrow is cast into the oven, shall He not much more clothe you, oh ye of little faith?" **(v. 30)**. If our Father is concerned enough to clothe the grass of the field which is short-lived, don't you think He is much more concerned about ensuring you have clothes to wear? Jesus reprimands us for failing to consider God's care—our lack of faith, our doubts, fears, and even our inability or refusal to exercise basic reasoning.

"Therefore, take no thought, saying, what shall we eat? Or; what shall we drink? Or, wherewithal shall we be clothed?" **(v. 31)**. Again, don't worry about where your next meal or clothing will come from.

"For after all these things do the gentiles seek: for your heavenly Father knoweth that you have need for all these things" **(v. 32)**. The whole world worries about these things, but our Father knows that you, His children, have need for these basics too.

"But seek ye first the Kingdom of God, and His righteousness; and all these things shall be added unto you" **(v. 33)**. What we need to do first is work toward the salvation of our souls by accepting Christ Jesus as our Savior, live our lives in obedience to our Father the best we can, and repent of our sins when we fail. Then as one of His children (believers), don't worry about anything because He will take care of us in accordance with His will.

"Take therefore no thought for the morrow; for the morrow shall take thought for the things of itself. Sufficient unto the day is the evil thereof" **(v. 34)**. In other words, don't waste time and energy worrying about tomorrow because evil will still be there, and ultimately, God works for the good of those who love Him even yesterday, today, and tomorrow.

> **I sought The Lord and He heard me, and delivered me from all my fears. They looked unto Him, and were lightened; and their faces were not ashamed. This poor man cried, and The Lord heard him, and saved him out of all his troubles. The Angel of The Lord encampeth round about them that fear Him, and delivereth them. (Psalms 34:4–7)**

When we look for the Lord, He answers us and will rescue us from our problems. When we look unto the Lord for answers, we find them, but when we look into ourselves, we find nothing but misery. The Lord hears us and will help us out of our troubles. The Lord provides His Holy Spirit to surround and protect from evil spirits those who revere, love, and worship Him.

> **I can do all things through Christ which strengtheneth me. (Philippians 4:13)**

> **Do not fear, I am with you, do not be dismayed, I am your God. I will strengthen you, I will help you, I will uphold you. (Isaiah 41:10)**

Families and Rearing Children God's Way

The responsibility of raising children is an undertaking requiring knowledge of God's Word, the Bible. This is His letter to us with instructions and examples as our Father demonstrating His love, patience, justice, and understanding to us, His own children. He is the perfect role model.

As with anything else, when we (man) try to do things our own way, we are likely to fail. It doesn't require another government study to discern the decline of our family unit in our country since the 1960s. It is a matter of record. We only have to look around us to see it collapsing before our very eyes. The examples are almost endless. The family unit is the essential fiber, which weaves us all together as one nation, providing the very strength and back bone of our country. We can see the beginning decline of our country even today, in part, as a result of our crumbling foundation—the family.

Properly raising children is the duty of responsible parenting. However, it is also the responsibility of grandparents, aunts, uncles, and others working in close proximity with our children. It is vital that we all work from the same page, in concert with God's teachings. Our children are one of God's greatest gifts entrusted to us, and we will all answer to Him with the result or lack thereof.

God warns us about the dangers of putting our faith in man's doctrines and philosophy.

> **See to it that no one takes you captive through hollow and deceptive philosophy, which**

> **depends on human tradition and the basic principles of this world rather than on Christ. (Colossians 2:8)**

The following selected instructions given to us by our heavenly Father isn't presented with any particular order in mind nor an exhaustive list by any means but rather a sampling of His wisdom revealed and often repeated for us throughout the entire Bible for emphasis sake.

Children learn what they live. Our example is imperative.

> **Command and teach these things. Don't let anyone look down on you because you are young, but set an example for the believers in speech, in life, in love, in faith, and in purity. (1 Timothy 4:11–12)**

Throughout this process, we will make mistakes, and when we do, it is important to openly admit them as an example to our children, then correct them, be consistent, and pray for each other.

> **Therefore confess your sins to each other and pray for each other so that you may be healed. The prayer of a righteous man is powerful and effective. (James 5:16)**

Our own conduct is constantly surveilled by our children; it's probably the easiest way for them to learn by our example.

> **"Do not let any unwholesome talk come out of your mouths, but only what is helpful for building others up according to their needs, that it may benefit those who listen" (Ephesians 5:29).**

Hostilities (wrath) displayed toward one another teaches our children aggression and fighting.

> **"A gentle answer turns away wrath, but a harsh word stirs up anger" (Proverbs 15:1).**

We must take precautions not to become or appear critical.

> **"Fathers, do not exasperate your children; instead, bring them up in the training and instruction of The Lord" (Ephesians 6:4).**

The Ten Commandments **(Exodus 20:3–17)** are the basis for all law condensed to their lowest denominator by our Lord. They must be taught to our children. And surprise—one of God's earliest promises can be found there which pertains directly to our children:

> **"Honor your father and your mother, so that you may live long in the land The Lord your God is giving you" (Exodus 20:12).**

Children must learn fairness in justice and to always do the right thing. Again, God is the standard of all righteousness to which we must aspire. One of the common modern phrases easy for children to remember is "What would Jesus do?"

> **He will judge the world in righteousness; He will govern the peoples with justice. The Lord is a refuge for the oppressed, a stronghold in times of trouble. Those who know Your Name will trust in You, for You, Lord, have never forsaken those who seek You. (Psalm 9:8–10)**

STUDY 10

It is necessary that our children know that we have certain expectations from them as they learn right from wrong, just as God requires of us.

> **"He has showed you, o man, what is good. And what does the Lord require of you? To act justly and to love mercy and to walk humbly with your God" (Micah 6:8).**

Our God is love;

> **"For God so loved the world that He gave His one and only Son, that whoever believes in Him shall not perish but have eternal life" (John 3:16).**

By His example, we too must love one another, even our enemies.

> **"But I tell you; love your enemies and pray for those who persecute you, that you may be sons of Your Father in heaven" (Matthew 5:44–45).**

Children must learn acceptance of others and must be taught how to love one another. This is something we must talk about aloud and with our children always.

> **Therefore, as God's chosen people, holy and dearly loved, clothe yourselves with compassion, kindness, humility, gentleness and patience. Bear with each other and forgive whatever grievances you may have against one another. Forgive as the Lord forgave you. And over all these virtues put on love, which binds them all together in perfect unity. (Colossians 3:12–14)**

Honesty—again, one of the very basic laws we learn from the Ten Commandments; **"Thou shall not bear false witness against your neighbor" (Exodus 20:16).** We don't lie and must always tell the truth. Think what the effects are when we tell our children such things as "Don't tell your mom" or "Don't tell your dad" or the "little white lie." Even our actions must also be honest.

> **Do not use dishonest standards when measuring length, weight or quantity. Use honest scales and honest weights, an honest ephah and an honest hin. I am The Lord Your God, who brought you out of Egypt. (Leviticus 39:35–37)**

When we visit the zoo, we take delight in feeding the animals. The same is true in the wild. During a particularly harsh winter, we feel almost honorable when we've laid out corn for the deer to eat. We've saved a life. They keep coming back for more each day and begin to expect it. To the extreme perhaps of the zoo-kept animals, they may no longer remember how to hunt their own food. So it is with man. If we don't teach our children life's lessons on what is expected of them, they are quick to learn entitlement even to the extreme of today where they feel society owes them a home, food, televisions, telephone, healthcare, etc. However, none of this is to be confused with legitimate and loving care and charity provided to the poor.

> **In the name of The Lord Jesus Christ, we command you, brothers, to keep away from every brother who is idle and does not live according to the teaching you received from us. For you yourselves know how you ought to follow our example. We were not idle when we were with you, nor did we eat anyone's food without paying for it. On the contrary, we worked night and day, laboring and toiling so that we would**

> **not be a burden to any of you. We did this not because we do not have the right to such help, but in order to make ourselves a model for you to follow. For even when we were with you, we gave you this rule; "If a man will not work, he shall not eat." (2 Thessalonians 3:6–10)**

We must always encourage our children to grow and continue our encouragement to one another.

> **For everything that was written in the past was written to teach us, so that through endurance and the encouragement of the scriptures we might have hope. May The God who gives endurance and encouragement give you a spirit of unity among yourselves as you follow Christ Jesus, so that with one heart and mouth you may glorify The God and Father of Our Lord Jesus Christ? (Romans 15: 4–6)**

> **For you know that we dealt with each of you as a father deals with his own children, encouraging, comforting, and urging you to live lives worthy of God, who calls you into His Kingdom and Glory. (1 Thessalonians 2:11–12)**

Above all, we must not give up teaching. It is a full-time job in everything we do whether it is literal written instruction or by our own living example. Most importantly, we must always remember to ask God for His help.

> **Do not be deceived: God cannot be mocked. A man reaps what he sows. The one who sows to please his sinful nature, from that nature will reap destruction; the one who sows to please**

> **The Spirit, from The Spirit will reap eternal life. Let us not become weary in doing good, for at the proper time we will reap a harvest if we do not give up. Therefore, as we have opportunity, let us do good to all people, especially to those who belong to the family of believers. (Galatians 6:7–10)**

Commit to the Lord. Have home interactive family Bible studies age-appropriate. Go to church as a family and become socially involved with other Christians and church family programs.

Talk about the Lord around the household as a course of daily conversation. Pray to our Father aloud as though He is sitting in the room with the family. Hold family meetings regularly to air problems and corrective actions as a family unit. Teach children to pray by having them write letters to their heavenly Father and talk to Him without "wish lists" and repetitious "chanting."

Humble yourselves before God—give Him credit.

> **And when the Chief Shepherd appears, you will receive the crown of glory that will never fade away. Young men, in the same way be submissive to those who are older. All of you, clothe yourselves with humility toward one another, because, God opposes the proud but gives grace to the humble. Humble yourselves, therefore, under God's mighty hand, that He may lift you up in due time. Cast all your anxiety on Him because He cares for you. (1 Peter 5:4–7)**

It is never too late to begin. Yesterday is history, tomorrow is a mystery, and today is a "present."

Worshiping God through Song and Music

God's children have been singing songs of joy to Him for eons of time as He tells us in His Word **(Job 38:7)**.

The delivery of worshiping God through song and music often brings forth displays of the sinful nature of man and his tendency to turn this presentation into a covetous, ego-controlled event rather than to the praise and glory of our heavenly Father.

Music and words relevant to this study such as *singing*, *to sing*, *singers*, *musical instruments*, and *musicians* obviously play an important role in worshiping our Father as we find references to them more than 278 times throughout scripture.

Singing and music are very important mediums with which God teaches us His message and for Christians to teach one another. Prayerfully, singing and music are also a medium which Christians use to express and return their love, praise, and thanksgiving to our heavenly Father **(Psalms 68:3–4)**.

In a spiritual setting such as church, where the Holy Spirit is among us, we sing praise to God with understanding the same as we pray to God with understanding **(1 Corinthians 14:15)**. We sing with a message of God's truths that all in fellowship will understand, meditate upon, and learn from.

> **Let the Word of Christ dwell in you richly in all wisdom, teaching, and admonishing [gently**

bring to mind] one another in psalms and hymns and spiritual songs, singing with grace [love] in your heart to the Lord. (Colossians 3:16)

Musicians present praises to God through the playing of musical instruments too **(2 Chronicles 30:21)**; instruments of all types are used—stringed instruments, cymbals, harps, and trumpets, etc. **(2 Chronicles 23:13, 9:11, 29:28; Psalms 68:25; Habakkuk 3:19)**.

We may even sing quietly to ourselves sacred songs, such as **Psalms chapter 115,** religious hymns, and other songs of a heavenly nature rather than a worldly one. In doing so, we keep our thoughts engaged in praise, honor, joy, love, power, mercy, happiness, and thanksgiving with reverence to our Lord **(Ephesians 5:19)**.

Those who overcome this sinful world and the tribulation of Satan's return as the antichrist without worshiping him and overcoming his name (sixth vial, sixth seal, sixth trump—666) will all join together and sing "The Song of Moses" found in **Deuteronomy 32:1–43**. We will also be singing "The Song of the Lamb" with the lyrics given in **Revelation 15:3–4**. These songs will be sung just prior to the new heaven and earth age when Jesus returns at His second advent **(Revelation 15:2–4)**.

Songs of worship are sung to the glory of our heavenly Father, not our own. Songs of worship are sung for His praise, not that of an audience. Songs of worship are sung as a continued ministry of His Word, understandable, and to teach one another of His love, of His mercy, of His Son, and His salvation given freely to all on the repentance of our sins **(Luke 13:1–9)** that "whosoever believeth on Him should not perish, but have everlasting life" **(John 3:16)**.

The Wife of Noble Character

Introduction

The book of the Proverbs of King Solomon, the son of David, King of Israel was penned circa 970 BC. When Solomon became king of Israel, he was about nineteen or twenty years old. At that time, he had asked God for wisdom in judging His people, which God granted. In fact, our heavenly Father was so pleased with Solomon's request for wisdom rather than wealth or power and honor that He gave him not only what he had asked, but He gave Solomon wisdom greater than any man before him or any man since. In addition to becoming the wisest man in history, God also adorned Solomon with the greatest wealth, power, and honor among all other kings of the day during his reign **(1 Kings 3:9–13)**. God told Solomon that *if* he would "walk in My ways, to keep My statutes and My commandments, as thy father David did walk, then I will lengthen thy days" **(1 Kings 3:14)**. Sadly, Solomon did not and died at approximately sixty years of age after a forty-year reign **(1 Kings 11:42)**.

Solomon's mother, Bath-sheba, loved her son very much. Her pet name for him was Lemuel. In the introduction to the book of Proverbs, he has advised us to "hear the instruction of thy father and mother and forsake not the law of thy mother" **(Proverbs 1:8)**. In other words, he is telling us to listen to the advice of your father and mother. "The law of thy mother" referenced is **Proverbs chapter 31** written to him by his mother. Within this chapter beginning in **Verse 8** is where we find her advice regarding the **"Wife of Noble Character."**

Who can find a virtuous woman? For her price is far above rubies. The heart of her husband doth safely trust in her, so that he shall have no need of spoil. She will do him good and not evil all the days of her life. She seeketh wool and flax and worketh willingly with her hands. She is like the merchant ships, she bringeth her food from afar. She riseth also while it is yet night and giveth meat to her household and a portion to her maidens. She consideth a field and buyeth it. With the fruit of her hands she planteth a vineyard. She girdeth her loins with strength and strengtheneth her arms. She perceiveth that her merchandise is good; her candle goeth not out by night. She layeth her hands to the spindle and her hands hold the distaff. She stretcheth out her hand to the poor; yes, she reacheth forth her hands to the needy. She is not afraid of the snow for her household; for all her household are clothed with scarlet. She maketh herself coverings of tapestry; her clothing is silk and purple. Her husband is known in the gate, where he sitteth among the elders of the land. She maketh linen and selleth it and delivereth girdles unto the merchant. Strength and honour are her clothing; and she shall rejoice in time to come. She openeth her mouth with wisdom; and in her tongue is the law of kindness. She looketh well to the ways of her household and eateth not the bread of idleness. Her children arise up and call her blessed; her husband also and he praiseth her. Many daughters have done virtuously, but thou excellest them all. Favour is deceitful, and beauty is vain; but a woman that feareth the Lord, she shall be praised. Give her of the fruit of her hands; and let her own works praise her in the gates.

STUDY 12

THE WIFE OF NOBLE CHARACTER
Proverbs 31:8

She makes linen garments and sells them and supplies the merchants with sashes.

She is clothed with strength and dignity A wife of noble character, who can find? She is worth far more than rubies.

Her husband has full confidence in her and lacks nothing of value. She brings him good not harm, all the days of her life.

She selects wool and flax and works with eager hands. She is like the merchant ships, bringing her food from afar. She gets up while it is still dark; she provides food for her family and portions for her servant girls.

She considers a field and buys it; out of her earnings she plants a vineyard. She sets about her work vigorously; her arms are strong for her tasks. She sees that her trading is profitable, and her lamp does not go out at night. In her hands she holds the distaff and grasps the spindle with fingers.

She opens her arms to the poor and extends her hands to the needy.

When it snows, she has no fear for her household; for all of them are clothed in scarlet. She makes coverings for her bed; she is clothed in fine linen and purple.

Her husband is respected at the city gate where he takes his seat among the elders of the land.

She is clothed with strength and dignity; She can laugh at the days to come. She speaks with wisdom and faithful instruction is on her tongue.

She watches over the affairs of her household and does not eat the bread of idleness. Her children arise and call her blessed; her husband also, and he praises her.

Many women do noble things, but you surpass them all.

Charm is deceptive, and beauty is fleeting; but a woman who has reverence for the Lord is to be praised. Give her the reward she has earned, and let her works bring her praise at the city gate.

Understanding Death

In Summary

The bigger picture we have to understand is this: God tells us He is the Alpha and the Omega, the beginning and the end, and He created His children, those who will love Him, to share eternity with Him.

We are all here on this earth to decide of our own freewill, whether we will love sinfulness and serve Satan or we will love righteousness and serve God.

These flesh bodies are just temporary vessels of clay housing our everlasting spiritual bodies. When we die, our spiritual body immediately enters paradise on one side of the gulf or the other depending on our actions while here on earth. In paradise, we await the beginning of the millennium period, a thousand-year period of teaching under Christ's iron rod of discipline.

At Christ's second coming to earth, all of us that are here at that time (good and bad) will be changed instantly into our spiritual bodies as flesh bodies can't enter heaven because it is in a different dimension. This marks the beginning of that millennium period after which we face the judgement of God's great white throne to receive our rewards—good or bad, an eternity of life or death.

As Christians, however, those who have accepted Christ as their Savior and have repented of their sins, we have nothing to fear. God has promised those who believe in His Son Jesus and accept Him as Savior will share eternity with Him. It is His free gift to us, not of good works but faith. As Christians, we are no different than anyone else when we sin and are also subject to eternal death; however as Christians, we are forgiven of our sins, and they are forgotten when we truly repent of them. Jesus paid the price for sin when He was nailed to the cross and died there for us.

To Begin

There are a couple of basic biblical teachings that must be recognized as components to the understanding of the death of our flesh bodies (i.e., their creation, purpose, and how to obtain eternal life) before we can comprehend what happens at our physical death, where we go, and why. We won't be going into a deep study of these components but will overview them here in order to understand the basic concepts.

Man's science accurately explains to us that our flesh bodies are made of organic materials found in the earth and mostly of water (H_2O) and that we must intake organic materials to sustain them as living organisms. As with any living organism, when it dies, it returns back to its primary components—without form, like dirt. The end.

Well, I assure you, our heavenly Father is not the God of the dead but is the God of the living. Let's begin.

Genesis 1:26–31 explains that God created man on the sixth day after "our image and likeness" to eat the organic foods and meats that He created for us, spelled out in detail in **Leviticus chapter 11**. With a little more detail into the creation of another man, which would establish the blood line from which Jesus Christ would eventually be born, **Genesis 2:4–25** tells us that on the eighth day God created the Adam man and Eve "from dust of the earth."

Who is the "our" mentioned above? This takes us into the study of the three earth and heaven ages—the one that was before (**2 Peter 2:5–8** and elsewhere) this second earth and heaven age **(Genesis 1:3 and beyond)** and the third heaven and earth age to come **(Revelation chapter 21)**. We existed in our spiritual bodies during the first earth age when God destroyed that earth age as it was then **(Genesis 1:1–2** when properly translated from Hebrew) and **(Job chapter 38, etc.)** when Satan rebelled and a third of God's children followed him in his fall from grace and were thrown out of heaven. Our souls and spiritual bodies remain with our flesh bodies during this, the second earth age. By the way, this is not a reincarnation thing. We continue our existence in our spiritual bodies in the third heaven and earth age too, for flesh and blood cannot enter heaven as it is in a different dimension **(1 Corinthians 15:50)**.

Yes, we have two bodies **(1 Corinthians 15:35–49)**—a flesh body which is affected by disease, sickness, age, and dies, and a spiritual body within us which is not affected by disease, sickness, age, or death (if found incorruptible).

God, as any loving father would be, is reluctant to destroy any of His children, which He created of His love for His pleasure. He is patient and longsuffering, desiring only that His children love Him in return **(Hosea 6:6)**. Love is something that cannot be bought, sold, or forced upon anyone. It comes only from a desiring heart. In this earth age, we must be "born again" ("from above" properly translated from the Greek) **(John 3:3, 5, 13)**. We must enter this earth age through the womb (water) to choose between following Satan or loving our Father and following Him. God gives us freewill to accomplish this, to choose good or evil without force. He wants those who love Him to dwell with Him for eternity, and those who don't await an eternal death of their spiritual souls. Life in these flesh bodies on earth is but a fleeting moment of time against forever. It is an interim phase for one purpose, of which each soul must pass through, that we might choose for ourselves who we will serve.

Our flesh bodies are weak and succumb to evil sin **(Ephesians 2:1–10)**. Therefore, God, full of love, grace, and forgiveness, **"sent His only begotten Son, that whosoever believeth in Him, shall not parish, but have everlasting life" (John 3:16).** Our eternal salvation is a free gift from God, made so easy that even a child can understand it. As believers, we should be unafraid of the physical death of our flesh bodies **(2 Corinthians 5:6–8)** or to stand before the judgement seat of Christ **(2 Corinthians 5:10)** if we have accepted Christ as our Savior **(1 Timothy 1:15)**, and with repentant hearts, we have asked for the forgiveness of our sins committed while in these flesh bodies **(Romans 3:20–25)**. This is *the* matter of eternal life or eternal death of our spiritual souls for which Jesus died on the cross for us that we might be saved **(Hebrews 9:11–15)**. Again, this simple choice is each of ours, but we must believe and accept Him, and when we do, God's blessings never end through eternity.

When our flesh body dies, we are finished with it. However, our soul, the intellect of our spiritual being, does not lie in a hole in the ground here on earth. If we believe that Christ rose again defeating death, then we must also believe that we too will rise upon the death of our flesh bodies. Our spiritual body and soul instantly returns to the Father which created it **(Ecclesiastes 12:6–7; 2 Corinthians 5:6–8)**. We are with Him in paradise on one side of the gulf or the other. Jesus gives us a picture of this in **Luke 16:19–31**. Here, we await God's judgement until after the millennium, a thousand-year period of teaching (this is a study for another time). For those of us still here on earth at the end of the tribulation periods of the end times and at the sounding of the seventh trumpet announcing Christ's return, all will (believers and nonbelievers alike) be changed from our flesh bodies to our spiritual bodies "in the twinkling of an eye" **(1 Corinthians 15:51–58)**.

Capital Punishment

The term *capital punishment* is defined as "the death penalty for a crime." The word *capital* means "very injurious or grave," and the word *punishment* refers to a "penalty imposed as for the transgression (violation) of law."

The purpose of this study is to reveal God's guidance from His Word, the Bible, in enacting the sentence of death upon an individual human being, a child of God, as the price to be paid for the very injurious and severe transgression of His commandment involving the murder of another one of his children; another human being.

God's Ten Commandments are found in **Exodus chapter 20**. The first five commandments pertain to laws of spiritual obedience, and the second five pertain to universal or civil law. While speaking to a lawyer who was tempting Jesus, the lawyer asked Jesus, "Which is the great commandment in the law?" **(Matthew 22:36)** and Jesus summed up both of these groups of the Ten Commandments into their lowest common denominators. For the first group (1 through 5), "Thou shalt love The Lord thy God with all thy heart, and with all thy soul, and with all thy mind." For the second group (6 through 10), "Thou shalt love thy neighbour as thyself" **(Matthew 22:37–39)**. Jesus concluded, adding, "On these two commandments hang all the law and the prophets" **(Matthew 22:40)**.

Jesus explains to us here that all of God's laws and teachings lie within these two commandments. How revealing God's Word becomes when we stop trying to complicate its simplicity.

The sixth commandment in most Bibles reads, "Thou shall not kill" **(Exodus 20:13)**. Because of this word *kill*, many consider this to be an all-encompassing command against taking the life of any human being under any circumstance in concert with Jesus's overwhelming message expressing brotherly love, forgiveness, and mercy toward one another.

The word *kill* has at least ten different meanings in the English language (i.e.; to cause the death of, slaughter for food, war, delete, turn off, etc.) with similar definitions in both the Hebrew and Greek languages.

However, the word *kill*, as written in **Exodus 20:13**, has been mistranslated from the original Hebrew language of the manuscripts. The original Hebrew word is *ratsach* which means "to murder" (Strong's Exhaustive Concordance of The Bible, word #7523). In the Greek language of the New Testament, the word is *phoneuo*, which means "a murderer, criminal, or intentional homicide" (Strong's Concordance word #5407 from the root #5406).

When properly translated, the sixth commandment reads, "Thou shalt not murder," which narrows our center of attention considerably. The word *murder* ("ratsach" and "phoneuo") is the unlawful, malicious, deliberate, lying-in-wait, intentional killing or homicide of one human being by another.

Murder is not the death of a human being caused by an accident or the result of temporary emotional insanity, etc. The Old Testament had varying ways to deal with these types of occurrences referred to as "cities of refuge" **(Deuteronomy 19:2–6)**. Even today, an act of murder may fall into different categories such as second- and third-degree murder, manslaughter, etc.

The penalty of death for the act of murder is brought forth in both the Old and New Testaments beginning with **Exodus 21:12.** "He that smiteth a man, so that he die, shall be surely put to death." In **Numbers 35:16–18**, note the examples of murder given in each verse here ends with "The murderer shall surely be put to death."

The death penalty may also be applicable to the crime of rape as shown in the examples given in **Deuteronomy 22:22–26**.

Jesus refers to the ramifications of murder in violation of the sixth commandment found in **Matthew 5:21** when He said, "Whosoever shall kill ["murder" properly translated] shall be in danger of the judgement." What is the "judgement" said by them of old time in accordance with the law? Death. Jesus is talking about the murderer being in danger of eternal death, the death of their soul as judged by God. **1 John 3:15** states, "Whosoever hateth his brother is a murderer and ye know that no murderer hath eternal life abiding in him." **Revelation 21: 8** tells us that "[m]urderers [among others] have their part in the lake which burneth with fire and brimstone; which is the second death," the eternal death of the soul.

"Moreover ye shall take no satisfaction [no ransom/redemption] for the life of a murderer which is guilty of death; but he shall be surely put to death" **(Numbers 35:31)**. In other words, we cannot give God a ransom for the murderer as only God can redeem a person's soul. That decision is not ours to make—we are not God, and only He makes that judgement.

We are not to feel any guilt or pity for the death sentence of a murderer; "Thine eye shall not pity him, but thou shalt put away the guilt of innocent blood from Israel, that it may go well with thee" **(Deuteronomy 19:13)**. God also explains, "And those which remain shall hear, and fear, and shall henceforth commit no more any such evil among you" **(Deuteronomy 19:20)**. Unfortunately, thirty-two of the fifty states maintain the death penalty for murder, but few exercise their law. Instead, the state often employs a "death-row" status of incarceration for convicted murderers which habitually results in their lifelong imprisonment. Where is the deterrent against murder in this system? There is little, if any.

BIBLE STUDIES 102

"Whom shall He teach knowledge? And whom shall He make to understand doctrine? Them that are weaned from the milk and drawn from the breast. For precept must be upon precept, precept upon precept; Line upon line, line upon line; here a little, there a little" (Isaiah 28:9-10).

God's Law and Grace

Law. The word is derived from Hebrew in origin and means to "point the way" or "point out."

Grace. Unmerited, divine merciful favor.

Biblical laws consist of four general areas:

1. *Commandments.* An order instructing moral conduct such as the Ten Commandments established by God and recorded in **Exodus chapter 20**.
2. *Statutes.* Established rules or laws defined in writing (verses common laws that are established more by customs than legislation). See the examples found in **Leviticus chapters 11 and 18**.
3. *Judgements.* Decisions rendered through discernment of governing laws such as the examples found in **Exodus chapters 21 to 22**, etc.
4. *Ordinances.* Ceremonial ritual as provided in **Exodus chapters 25 to 27**, etc.

God's first commandment or order to man is found some four thousand years BC from the garden of Eden in G**enesis 2:16–17**. The transgression or violation of this commandment by man brought sin and death into the world. Sin is the transgression or violation of the laws of God **(1 John 3:4)**. The wages of sin is death **(Romans 6:23).**

Approximately thirty-four laws given by God are present in the book of Genesis and later reaffirmed in the Mosaic Code, such as the laws governing the Sabbath **(Genesis 2:3)** and murder **(Genesis 9:5–6)**. Interestingly too, we see some of God's divine laws of universal order also introduced to man in the book of Genesis, such as the laws of nature and laws of the universe.

From both scientific discovery and biblical records, it is known that alongside God's laws, prior to Sinai, the Babylonian laws, written by man, also existed approximately eight hundred years before the time of Moses. Known as the Code of Amraphel (Khammuraen), the latest date of these writings is believed to be 2139 BC. These earlier written laws were discovered by M.J. de Morgan in 1901. The existence of the Code of Amraphel law is revealed in biblical references such as **Genesis 14:1**. The Code of Amraphel governed the peoples living in an area from the Persian Gulf to the Caspian Sea and from Persia to the Mediterranean Sea and was enforced throughout Canaan at that time. The Amraphel laws are shown operating in **Genesis 15: 2**, as the law of adoption by Abram's heir, Eliezer. The punishments for violation of these laws were very severe, such as demonstrated in **Genesis 31:32**, where death is the punishment for the crime of stealing. There are several other examples of the known governing Code of Amraphel that had been established during the time of Genesis even though there is no record of their delivery.

The Mosaic Law, or Pentateuch, is most often referred to as the "Book of Moses," "Book of the Law," or "the Law of Moses." Although divinely authored by God, it is not penned by Moses alone. It also includes additions by Joshua (see **Joshua 24:26**) who doubtlessly also added **chapter 34** in the book of **Deuteronomy**. Samuel is recorded in **Isaiah 10:25** as having written in "the book." The "Book of Moses" consists of the first five books of the Bible—**Genesis, Exodus, Leviticus, Numbers,** and **Deuteronomy.**

The ordinances exclusively instruct, define, and lay out the ceremonial and ritual processes ruling over offerings and sacrifices presented by God's people at the altar, which was strictly administered by the priests of the tabernacle for the forgiveness and remission of sins as detailed in **Exodus chapter 35**, for example.

A good example of statutes is in **Leviticus chapter 11**, commonly referred to as the "Levitical food laws." In these laws, God "points the way" on how man will best preserve these flesh bodies in a good state of health with the foods we should and should not eat. The intent is that we lower the risk of illnesses and diseases from causing an early demise of these fragile entities, which are created from the elements of the earth, after all **(Genesis 2:7)**.

God provided legal guidance or judgements as seen in **Exodus chapters 21 to 23** for the Hebrew people entering the wilderness, after being freed from Egyptian control.

As a side note, **Numbers 2:32** sums the total of able bodied men from all the tribes of Israel to create an army for their self-protection at 603,550. When we add children, women, and the elderly, an estimated total Hebrew population at that time could be approximately 2.1 million people, equal to the population of Houston, Texas in 2012.

In the "Book of Moses," God "points the way" for everything his people will need to direct and guide their lives—even how to keep the camp of their army clean by keeping the use of latrines, whores, and homosexuals out of the camp **(Deuteronomy 23:9–18)**.

As an overview, we can see the love and protection God provides for His people in every imaginable detail throughout the Pentateuch, chapter by chapter, verse by verse. God's concerns and patience as a loving Father toward His children are also witnessed firsthand throughout the Old Testament under the covenant (contract) He made with Abram **(Genesis chapter 17)**, approximately 1871 years before the arrival of Emanuel (Jesus), meaning "God with us," as foretold in **Zechariah 9:9** and many other places throughout the Old Testament.

However, in the book of **Isaiah chapter 1**, God tells His people that He is tired of their vain daily oblations, sacrifices, and burnt offerings. They no longer mean anything to Him because of their continued iniquities (sinning).

Eventually, God disavowed His covenant with Israel and turned away from them, His chosen people. He saw His people no longer loved Him like their fathers before them, as demonstrated by their actions of continued wickedness, disobedience, idolatry, and refusal to walk in His statutes and judgements as a people **(Ezekiel chapter 5)**.

STUDY 1

Then in **Malachi 3:1–4,** God tells of His new covenant, transitioning "the Law of Moses" to the new covenant of Jesus Christ. The new covenant is also prophesized in **Zechariah chapter 11.**

The New Testament begins with **the book of Matthew** and brings forward the lineage of Jesus Christ, sets forth the Lord as Jehovah's King, and His claims as the Messiah, sent to fulfill all prophecies of the Old Testament concerning Him (read **Jeremiah 23:5–6**).

Jesus's message is very clear to the world in **Matthew 5:17–19.** Jesus didn't come to destroy "the law" or "the prophets" but to "fulfill." **Verse 18** reads:

> **For verily I say unto you, till heaven and earth pass, one jot [meaning smallest character in the Hebrew alphabet] or one tittle [meaning a mark over top a Hebrew letter or abbreviation] shall in no way pass from the law, till all be fulfilled.**

Continuing in **Matthew 5:21–48,** Jesus goes on to transcend (go beyond human knowledge) the Laws of Moses regarding murder (sixth commandment), adultery (seventh commandment), perjury (third commandment), retaliation **(Exodus 21:25; Leviticus 24:20; Deuteronomy 19:21),** and love **(Leviticus 19:18).**

Jesus's death on the cross for our sins "blotted the hand writing of the ordinances" or did away with the blood ordinances of the Law of Moses **(Colossians 2:11–14).**

Hebrews chapter 9 details that Christ became our sanctuary and sacrifice of blood ordinance and why, summed up in the last verse **(28)**: "So Christ was once offered to bear the sins of many; and unto them that look for Him shall He appear the second time without sin, unto salvation."

In **Hebrews 10:8–10,** Jesus reiterates what God had said, that He "wasn't pleased with the sacrifice and offerings and burnt offerings for sin which are offered by the law," and Jesus said, "I come to do Thy will, oh God." Jesus takes away the first (a sacrificial offering for sin) so that He may establish the second (God's will). "[B]y the which will we are sanctified [purified and free from sin] through the offering of the body of Jesus Christ once and for all" (**v. 10**).

So at this point, we see that Jesus, in obedience with God's will, is our offering, sanctuary, and sacrifice for sin, replacing the blood ordinances, statutes, and judgements pertaining to the remission of sin as established under the Law of Moses. Other than that, Jesus declared He did not come to change one thing regarding God's laws, such as the laws governing love, worship, food, moral conduct, of the universe, nature, etc. In fact, Jesus actually teaches a defined "transcending" detail of God's laws, providing a more simplified understanding of their interrelationship with one another to their lowest common denominator when the disciples asked; "Master, which is the greatest commandment in the law?" (**Matthew 26:32**) And Jesus replies,

> **Thou shalt love the Lord thy God with all thy heart, and with all thy soul, and with all thy mind. This is the first and great commandant. And the second is like unto it, thou shalt love thy neighbor as thyself. On these two commandments hang all the law and prophets. (Matthew 26:37–40)**

Think about it: yes, we are still under "the law."
God establishes the new covenant in **Hebrews 10:16–18**:

> **This is the covenant that I will make with them after those days saith the Lord; I will put My laws into their hearts, and in their minds will I write them. And their sins and iniquities will I remember no more. Now where remission [forgiveness of sin] of these is, there is no more offering for sin.**

STUDY 1

The Lord is not slack concerning His promise, as some men count slackness; but is longsuffering [patient] to us-ward, not willing that any should perish, but that all should come to repentance. (2 Peter 3:9)

In **Romans 3:19–31**, God explains to us that all of mankind is under the law, and as such, no one is excused in His sight, for by the law is knowledge of sin, for all have sinned and come short of the glory of God but are freely forgiven by God's grace (unmerited, divine merciful favor) through the redemption (deliverance from sin) that is in Jesus Christ. Through the atonement (appeasement) through faith in the blood of Jesus (his death on the cross) are we, believers in Jesus, both Jews and gentiles, forgiven or justified of our sins in God's eyes. This is the law of faith. Is the law voided through faith? Quite the opposite, the law is established by faith.

In other words, faith establishes the law that identifies sins, which can be forgiven by repentance (God's grace).

"What then? Shall we sin, because we are not under the law, but under grace? God forbid!" **(Romans 6:15).** Is it not a violation of God's laws to steal (eighth commandment), murder (sixth commandment), lie (ninth commandment), etc.?

Under God's new covenant with man, through Jesus Christ, we can see that law and grace work hand in hand, one with the other. One does not exist without the other.

"For God so loved the world, that He gave His only begotten Son, that whosoever believeth in Him should not perish, but have everlasting life" **(John 3:16).**

The Three Earth and Heaven Ages

Introduction

In this examination of God's Word, we will touch upon a few subjects where it will be helpful if we have a basic understanding of some biblical principles in order to keep the focus of our topic as concise as possible.

God wrote His letter to us, the Bible, to teach us all things **(Mark 13:25)** that we might know, understand, and love Him as He loves us. His Word presents many subjects for the collective purpose of supporting His most important message of salvation that we might share eternity with Him **(John 3:16)**.

As Christian believers, our Father requires we take the first step by having faith in Him **(Hebrews 11:6)**. To have reverence for and to love the Lord is the beginning of all knowledge **(Proverbs 1:7)**. In order to begin our search for His truths, we have to *read* the Bible **(2 Timothy 2:15)**. We must put forth the effort of *study* in order to fully appreciate the depth of instruction presented to us **(2 Timothy 2:7)**. Many Christians have acquired biblical basics and a fundamental zeal for God but no real knowledge **(Romans 10:2)**. Most Christians never go beyond biblical basics or "milk" and remain unskilled with a minimal understanding of the Bible when our knowledge should be as "meat" so that we will teach our families and others **(Hebrews 5:12–15)**.

In addition to our Father's written Word, He sent us His Son Jesus who experienced life and death in these flesh bodies on earth that He might teach us by His example. God doesn't ask us to do anything He Himself would not do. After Jesus's return home, our Father continues to support our learning today by providing His Holy Spirit teaching us all things and bringing them to our remembrance **(John 14:25–26)**. With all our heavenly Father has sacrificed out of His love for us, it hardly seems that a little effort on our part to simply *read* and *study* is so much to ask of us.

An understanding of the three earth and heaven ages I describe as the "mortar," which holds other building blocks of the Bible together. The result is a more comprehensive path to clarifying and understanding the mysteries of God's truths. The fact is if we don't understand the beginning, we'll never understand the end.

The First Earth and Heaven Age

"In the beginning, God created the heaven and the earth" **(Genesis 1:1)**.

Nowhere in the Bible does God provide a specific time as to when He completed this task, simply that He did, which is repeated again in His conversation with Job **(Job 38:4).**

Time is a component quantity of various measurements used to sequence events on earth. Time is also the infinite continued progress of existence as defined by man's finite processing abilities. I don't think time means anything to our Father except it's relevancy to us in this here and now. Time is certainly measured differently by God as explained in **2 Peter 3:8;** for every thousand years of our measurement is the equal of one day to our Father. God states He "is the Alpha and Omega" **(Revelation 1:8)**, meaning the first of anything and the end.

Our sciences today demonstrate through various means that this earth is "eons" old, meaning an incalculable period of time. Some dinosaur fossils have been determined to be as old as two hundred thirty-one million years! We are told by scientists the ice age began about forty million years ago and technically still exists with the north and south ice caps in comparison to the "time that was," when dinosaurs ate buttercups in Alaska amidst palm trees.

The Bible does not contradict these events or an earth that is eons old. The Bible uses terms describing the heaven and earth as "works of old" **(Proverbs 8:22)** or as "days of old" **(2 Peter 3:5)**. These phrases are given to three definitions in the Hebrew language according to *The Strong's Concordance of the Bible* (see addendum) as follows—beginning of the world (word 5769); old, world without end, perpetual (word 5703); and antiquity or old (word 6924). In the Greek language of the New Testament, the definitions are primeval, belonging to the first ages, primitive, old time (word 744); of old (word 1597); origin (word 1537); and another form(word 3819).

God created this earth to be inhabited, whether it was the first earth age, this earth age, or the new earth age which follows in the future. It is the same earth, just different dispensations or periods of time.

> **For thus saith the Lord that created the heavens; God Himself that formed the earth and made it; He hath established it. He created it not in vain [Hebrew "tohu," meaning without form]. He formed it to be inhabited; I am The Lord and there is none other. (Isaiah 45:18)**

God also created His children (the angels) to live with Him from the beginning, "when all the morning stars [Hebrew figure of speech meaning things represented as persons] sang together and all the sons of God [spiritual creations not of flesh—angels] shouted for joy" **(Job 38:4–7; Proverbs 8:22–31)**.

We have two bodies, both a flesh body and a spiritual body which is within us **(1 Corinthians 15:35–49)**. When our flesh body dies, our spiritual body immediately returns to the Father who created it **(Ecclesiastes 12:6–7)**. Flesh cannot enter heaven as it is a different dimension **(1 Corinthians 15:50)**. However, even when God created the flesh man, He created us in the very image of our spiritual being and of the angels and even of our Father Himself **(Genesis 1:26–27)**. Thousands of years later when the disciples (Phillip in particular) asked Jesus what the Father looks like, Jesus replied, "[H]e that hath seen me hath seen the Father" **(John 14:9; John 10:30)**.

In the first earth age, Satan had been created by our Father as a cherub (a supernatural being), the perfect pattern, and grew in stature guarding the mercy seat until his pride caused him to sin, placing him in an adversarial position against God **(Ezekiel 28:12–17)**. This rebellion on Satan's part so angered our Father that He cast Satan and his followers, one-third of God's children, down to earth **(Revelation 12:1–4)**. This period in time in which God cast Satan and his followers down to the earth is called the "katabolle." Katabolle is Greek (word 2598) meaning to throw down, cast down, descend, or fall. Jesus was witness to Satan's fall from heaven as He states in **Luke 10:18**.

The word *foundation* in Hebrew (word 3245) means "established" and has been incorrectly translated several times in the King James Version (KJV) Bible. This is important as the Greek "themelios" (word 2310) is translated as "foundation" and means—a foundation to build upon, while the Greek "katabole" (word 2602 with one *l*) has also been translated as "foundation" when it's root word is "katabolle" (word 2598 with two *l*s), meaning a deposition or removal from an office or position as correctly used in the preceding paragraph. This is important to note as this defines two separate periods of time—the "themelios" or literal foundation of the world as in **Genesis 1:1** and the "katabolle," describing Satan's fall from God's grace which occurred after the "themelios" or founding of the world and before this present earth age as we will see.

For Satan's rebellious actions and sins, God sentenced him to death **(Ezekiel 28:17–19)**. Needless to say, our Father could not destroy one-third of His children; what father could? Instead, God, full of anger, shook and destroyed the earth to the stage where it was without form and a desolate ruin. There were no birds, no man, or cities any longer in existence. Yes, there were even cities in the first earth age **(Jeremiah 4:19–28)**. The earth that was, now covered with water, "perished" (Greek word 622) meaning in composition ruin, destroyed, die, death **(2 Peter 3:6)**. Scientists see the evidence of catastrophic events including earthquakes, volcanic eruptions, asteroids colliding with the earth, and world flooding in geological studies of the earth's crust today and also the shifting of the earth's axis. "I beheld the mountains, and, lo, they trembled, and all the hills moved lightly" **(Jeremiah 4:24)**. God has given us a picture of what he did to the first earth age. Once again referencing man's sciences, it is theorized that today's continents were at one time a single land mass which began to shift to become the continents we know today. Have we just read about this occurrence written in God's Word long before man was capable of theorizing such hypotheses?

As we were in our spiritual bodies during the first earth age, no fossils of man are ever found as are the fossils of dinosaurs during that earlier time two hundred thirty-one million or more years ago. Fossils of flesh man are only about eight thousand years old, which coincides with the sixth-day creation recorded later in **Genesis chapter 1**. We also find fossils of other flesh animals, fish, birds, and plants, etc., which were in existence during the first earth age, in support of our sciences of today.

We need to make clear at this point that this total death and ruin of the world, including every living thing on the earth, and worldwide flooding cannot be confused with the flood waters brought about in Noah's time as recorded in **Genesis chapters 6 to 8**. Noah's stages of flooding lasted two hundred four days **(Genesis 8:3, 6, 10, 12)** and covered one full year from beginning to end as measured against Noah's age starting when he was six hundred years old **(Genesis 7:6)** and ending when he turned six hundred one years old **(Genesis 8:13)**. In addition, Noah, his wife, family, and two of every flesh aboard the ark survived and replenished the earth **(Genesis 9:1)**. Remember, nothing survived the destruction of the first earth age.

So what have we learned so far? (1) God created the heavens and earth eons ago strategically established in a perfect environment; (2) God created the earth to be inhabited by Himself, His children (serving angels of spiritual bodies), and flesh creatures large and small to the joy of all His creations; (3) God destroyed this first earth age due to Satan's rebellion and sin which brought about the "katabolle." (4) The records of biblical events and established sciences do not contradict one another in principle when confirming that the creation of the earth was billions of years ago and the calamitous destruction of the first earth age millions of years ago with an uncertain passing of time between the two events and that the earth is not a mere six thousand years old as many would have you think.

Now let's begin with the second verse of the Bible and the first mistranslated Hebrew word into English.

The Second Earth and Heaven Age

"And the earth **was** without form, and void, and darkness **was** upon the face of the deep and the spirit of God moved upon the face of the water" **(Genesis 1:2)**.

For the sake of brevity in this study, suffice it to say that the word *was*, as used in this verse, does not exist in the Hebrew language (see addendum for details). The word written in the original Hebrew manuscripts is *hayah*, pronounced "haw-yaw" (word 1961), and when correctly translated means to exist, (i.e., be, become, come to pass, or became).

When correctly translated to English from the Hebrew manuscripts, this verse will now read: "And the earth **became** without form, and void, and darkness **came** upon the face of the deep and the Spirit of God moved upon the face of the water."

We have already learned that God did not create the earth "without form" (word 8414; Hebrew "tohu," meaning desolation, to lie in waste) and "void" (word 922; Hebrew meaning undistinguishable ruin). But we can see that "the earth became desolate and an undistinguishable ruin" following the "katabolle" which occurred after the initial creation millions or maybe even billions of year earlier.

A very natural question following an appropriately translated verse of **Genesis 1:2** comes to mind by most of us at this point which is "What was the earth before if it *became* a desolate waste and an undistinguishable ruin?" If **Genesis 1:2** had been correctly translated from the start, matters of understanding would certainly be different today. For example, how many additional believers do you think there might be? How far would the theory of evolution have gone?

From **Genesis 1:3–31**, God is involved with the recording of the rebuilding of the earth, the second earth age, which remembering **2 Peter 3:8** (a thousand years to man is 1 day to with the Lord), these "six days" of the Lord equals six thousand years to man. God rested on the seventh day (a thousand years) and on the eighth day (adding another thousand years for man) He created Adam and Eve, the bloodline from which Jesus would come. When we include an additional two thousand years since the death of Jesus, we can estimate with relative accuracy, this second earth age to be approximately twelve thousand to thirteen thousand years old (see chronology of events in the addendum).

Why are we here in this earth age? Because of God's love for us, He couldn't just "zap" one-third of His children to death.

Our heavenly Father has provided us with freewill to decide individually whom we will follow—Satan and evil or God and righteousness. Who do we love? Our Father knows that love is something you can't buy or force upon anyone. It is something that must come from the heart, otherwise it's not love. He wants His children to love Him as He loves us by our own choosing.

Jesus tells us that "except a man is born again, he cannot see the kingdom of God" **(John 3:3)**. There is a mistranslation here with the word *again* in this sentence. The Greek word (word 509) used here is *anothen*, meaning "above." All of God's children must be "born from above." Jesus continues, "[A]nd no man hath ascended up to heaven, but he that came down from heaven, even the Son of Man which is in heaven" **(John 3:13)**. Again, God does not ask of us anything that He Himself wouldn't do. Jesus, who was in the beginning **(John 1:1)**, was also made flesh just like us and dwelt among us, the only begotten Son of the Father **(John 1:14)**. Likewise, we will pass from this earth in death only once; "and it is appointed unto men once to die, but after this the judgment" **(Hebrews 9:27)**. But for God's children, those who choose to love Him and repent of our sins, God promises life eternal **(John 3:16)**. When this flesh body dies, our spiritual body immediately returns to the Father that created it **(Ecclesiastes 12:6–7)**. If we believe that Jesus died and rose again, then we must believe that we too will also rise after our flesh bodies die **(1 Thessalonians 4:14)**. After all, isn't that the bottom line as to what Christianity is all about? If we don't believe Christ died for our sins and rose again, then we are not Christians. Christianity is a reality, not a religion. Jesus came into this earth age in flesh and blood to defeat death (Satan) so that we would not fear death and to experience life here on earth, including worldly temptations just as we do in the flesh, and to aid, relieve, and help us, His brethren **(Hebrews 2:14–18)**.

Each of us as spiritual beings must pass through this earth age for a short time within flesh bodies for the purpose of determining whether or not we will love our Father, including the one-third of His children which initially followed Satan in the katabolle. Eternal life or eternal death are our choices, and it will be one or the other. Our Father even gives us every tool imaginable to help us along the way—his letter of instructions (the Bible) telling us how to live in these flesh bodies, His Holy Spirit to guide, teach, and direct our daily lives **(John 14:26)**, and a private line of direct communication with Him through prayer anytime we want or need Him 24-7 **(Hebrews 4:16)**. God even provided His own Son as a living example for us to follow and a one-time atonement to forgive, pardon, and cancel any and all of our previous sins against Him when we repent of them—tell Him we're sorry. All He wants in return is our love as He loves us **(Hosea 6:6)**.

The future of this, the second earth age, is well established in both the New and Old Testament prophecies. A careful study of the "end times" is far too expansive of a project to document here and must be reserved for another time. However, it is essential to provide an overview of major events in order to seamlessly enter into the third earth and heaven age to follow.

Satan and his angels will be cast out of heaven onto the earth which marks the beginning of the end of this second earth age **(Revelation 12:7–9)**. Satan comes peacefully and prosperously **(Daniel 11:21)**. Satan comes as "anti" christ (Greek word 473, meaning "instead" of Christ) at the sixth vial **(Revelation 16:12–**

16), sixth seal **(Revelation 6:12–17)**, and sixth trump **(Revelation 9:11–13)**.

> **Here is wisdom. Let him that hath understanding count the number of the beast; for it is the number of a man; and his number is six hundred, threescore and six (666). (Revelation 13:18)**

Time has now run out for this earth age **(Revelation 10:6)**. The second advent of Jesus arrives on the seventh trump **(Revelation 11:15–19)**. As the seventh angel begins to sound the seventh trump, the mystery of God is finished as He had declared to His prophets **(Revelation 10:7)**. Note here that Satan comes before Christ on the sixth trump, and Jesus does not return until the seventh trump. Don't be deceived! Satan comes first (six comes before seven), pretending to be our Savior Jesus Christ.

The New Testament book of **Mark chapter 13** is a narrative by Jesus of the end times to the disciples. Parallel writings of the same can be read in **Matthew chapter 24** and **Luke chapter 21** as well. Brief summaries of all three earths and heaven ages are brought forth in **2 Peter chapter 3** and **Revelation chapter 12** for additional reading.

God established the earth perfect for His and our home (habitation) amidst the entire universe as its backdrop. Corrections were made necessary because of sin, but our Father returns the earth back to its initial state of perfection only better than ever because there will no longer be any sin **(Revelation chapter 21)**.

The triumphant return of Jesus to the earth marks the beginning of the millennium period. Satan is subdued, chained, and cast into the bottomless pit by Michael, shut up, and sealed to prevent him from deceiving anyone else until this millennium period is completed **(Revelation 20:1–10)**. The millennium is a period of teaching for those who otherwise never had the opportunity to learn of God's truths and salvation **(Ezekiel 44:23–24)**. Those who have already overcome judgment (repentant believers) will reign with Christ for this thousand-year period. This is the first resurrection.

STUDY 2

More information on the millennial period is found in **(Ezekiel chapters 40–48)**. At the end of the thousand-year period, Satan is released for the last time. He and his followers, those not found in the book of life subsequent to the second resurrection and the great white throne judgment, are sentenced to death and cast into the lake of fire **(Revelation 20:7–15)**. We are all judged "according to our works" **(Revelation 20:12–13)**. God's judgement is also a time of great joy as deserved rewards for our good works are also received as have been recorded in the book of life **(Matthew 16:27)**.

The Bible does not provide a tremendous amount of detailed information pertaining to the third earth age the same as it does not regarding the first earth age. Perhaps Jesus provides the reasoning of this purpose by our Father when in reply to Nicodemus, Jesus said, "If I have told you of earthly things, and ye believe not, how shall ye believe, if I tell you of heavenly things?" **(John 3:12)** However, as we saw regarding the first earth age, our Father has seen fit to also provide sufficient facts for our understanding of the third earth age, now rejoined with heaven right here.

This begins when the disciple John was taken in the spirit (another dimension) to view the future and told by God to write what he saw and to disseminate this information to the seven churches of Asia **(Revelation 1:10–11)**.

Within the last two chapters of the Bible **(Revelation chapters 21 and 22)**, John describes to us some exciting information about the third earth and heaven age to come. Same earth and heaven but made "new" (Greek word 2537 *kainos*, meaning freshness or refreshed).

The first thing John notices is that there is no longer any seas **(Revelation 21:1)**. A lot of speculation possible here, but one that is certain is a lot more "terra firma" will be available as about 71 percent of the earth's surface is currently covered by the seas.

Next, John sees the Holy City Jerusalem coming down from God out of heaven, God's tabernacle or the temple throne of God, where He Himself will dwell with His children as He had promised a few thousand years earlier **(Zechariah 2:10–12)**. Wherever God is, is His throne, is heaven. John gives a detailed description of God's temple but first reports on the more important decrees established by our Father's caring love surrounding our eternal wellbeing.

Our Father instantly wipes away all tears from His children's eyes and tells us there will be no more death, sadness, crying, or pain. These things are gone forever **(Revelation 21:4)**. God says it is done, reinforcing the finality of the old with His pledge to make all things new, restating the fact that He is the beginning and the end. God reassures each of us that have overcome evil He freely gives life eternal and that each shall be His heir in all things. He will be our God, and we will be His son **(Revelation 21:5–7)**!

Our Father further ensures our eternal wellbeing by removing all evil nonbelievers, murderers, whoremongers, sorcerers (Greek word 5332 *pharmakeus,* in this instance meaning spell-giving poisoner or drug pushers), idol worshippers, liars, and the *abominable* to the lake of fire, which is the second death **(Revelation 21:8)**.

Examples of persons doing things God finds as *abominable* is the utilization of diverse weights/cheaters **(Deuteronomy 25:13–16)**, worshippers of witchcraft, astrology, child sacrifice **(Deuteronomy 18:10–15)**, the disobedient, unruly **(Proverbs 3:32)**, homosexuality **(Leviticus 18:22)**, pridefulness, those with wicked imaginations and quick to perform mischief, false witnessing, those who sow discord **(Proverbs 6:16–19)**, and those who justify wickedness and condemn the just **(Proverbs 17:15).**

In addition to the aforementioned, other unrepentant persons who will not enter the kingdom of God are those involved in adultery, fornication, lasciviousness, hatred, wrath, heresies, jealousy, and drunkenness **(Galatians 5:19–21)**.

An angel took John high on a mountain to watch as God's temple descended from heaven and settle on earth. The structure is approximately fourteen hundred miles cubed and appeared as pure gold likened to clear glass, with twelve gates of pearl, three on each side for each of the twelve tribes of Israel. The temple is surrounded by a wall approximately two hundred eighty-feet tall, the color of jasper with one foundation layer for each of the twelve disciples, each garnished with all types of precious stones such as sapphire, jasper, emerald, beryl, topaz, amethyst, and more. The street therein is of pure gold as it were transparent glass. No moon or sun is needed for light as the glory of God and Jesus provided the light within. Only those listed in the Book of Life are able to enter in. Flowing out of the temple is a pure river of water of life as clear as crystal. On each side of the river is a tree of life, which bears twelve fruits for the enjoyment of the citizens, and the leaves of the tree are for the healing or health of the nations **(Revelation chapters 21–22)**.

> **I am the Alpha and the Omega, the Beginning and the End, the First and the Last. (Revelation 22:13)**
>
> **The Grace of Our Lord Jesus Christ be with you all. Amen. (Revelation 22:21)**

Addendum

"Was"

In the English definition, it is first- and third-person singular and the past indicative of "be."

When correctly translated from the Hebrew manuscripts, the original Hebrew word written in Genesis 1:2 is *hayah* (pronounced "haw-yaw"), which means to exist (i.e., be, become, come to pass, or as used in Genesis 1:2, "became"). The word *was* does not exist in the Hebrew language.

When the revisers of the English version Bible translated the original Authorized Version of the King James Bible in 1611, which had the word in italics, they decided that all italicized words of the manuscripts (carried through the Latin Vulgate of 1534 and Geneva Bible of 1560), which are plainly applied to the Hebrew but require additional words in the English, be printed in common type. They had now failed to distinguish the difference between the verb "to be" from the verb "to become" so that the lessons conveyed by the Authorized Version of the King James Bible are lost.

The Strong's Concordance of the Bible

The Strong's Concordance was first published in 1890, compiled by Dr. James Strong with the help of more than a hundred linguists who spent more than thirty-five years preparing it. *The Strong's Concordance* translates each word written in the King James Authorized Version of 1611 Bible back to the original languages as found in the Masoretic Hebrew Old Testament text and the Greek-received New Testament text including a defining dictionary of the

STUDY 2

original Hebrew/Chaldees or Greek word. Because of this work, we no longer have to be fluent in the Hebrew, Chaldees, or Greek languages of old.

Translate Verses Interpret

These two words are often interchanged back and forth incorrectly and may cause great confusion. They must be used with caution as even the lesser definitions of both words will include the word *interpret*, only adding more misunderstanding and uncertainty. For assistance in clarification, the English definition of both words is presented.

Interpret

1. To give the meaning of; explain, or construe.
2. To judge in a personal way.
3. To restate orally in one language what is said in another.

Translate

1. To express in another language.
2. Change into another language.
3. To explain in another language.
4. Interpret.

A Chronology in Time of Some Historical Events from the Beginning of this Earth Age

10000 BC	The creation of this, the second earth age
6000 BC	Man created (human kind, the races)
4004 BC	Adam and Eve created (the bloodline of Jesus)
2348 BC	Noah's flood
1490 BC	Hebrew manuscripts (Law of Moses) Old Testament
649 BC	The prophet Jeremiah is born

BIBLE STUDIES 102

4 BC	The birth of Jesus
AD 570	Islamic prophet Muhammad born
AD 1000	Leif Erikson discovered Newfoundland
AD 1095	Crusades fought
AD 1492	Columbus arrives in the Americas
AD 1776	The United States of America established
AD 1865	War between states ended
AD 1918	World War I ended
AD 1948	Israel recognized as a sovereign state by the world
AD 2017	(approximately twelve thousand to thirteen thousand years total)

The Kenites— Children of Satan

The exact location of the garden of Eden is unknown, and anything else is pure speculation; however, the Bible does provide some clues **(Genesis 2:10)**. The Bible states that a river which was used to water the garden flowed to a point where it parted into the head waters of four other rivers—the Pison, Gihon, Hiddekel (today's Tigres), and the Euphrates Rivers **(Genesis 2:10–14)**. Modern geography identifies this area as today's Armenia, bordering northeast Turkey.

Armenia is nearly centered between Russia to the north, Asia Minor and Asia to the east, Europe to the west, and the twenty-two countries to the south that make up today's Middle East. Armenia is home to the Caucasus mountain range and shares Mount Ararat, Noah's point of landing **(Genesis 8:4)** with the borders of northern Iran and southeast Turkey. Armenia has a long history as a Christian nation amidst its Islamic neighbors.

This region is also considered northern Mesopotamia. Mesopotamia is dubbed "the cradle of western civilization," home to the historical beginnings of scientific, mathematical, and written communications. Mesopotamia is recorded by name very early on in the Bible **(Genesis 24:10)** and is also recognized interchangeably as northeast Arabia.

God's creation of this current earth age is recorded in the book of **Genesis chapters 1 and 2**, which is a study unto itself for another time. However, to gain understanding of the broader picture of this study, an overview of some events within the garden of Eden follow to refresh our memories and establish our point of beginning.

God created "man" (Hebrew "adam," meaning mankind/human races) on the sixth day of creation **(Genesis 1:26–31)** about six thousand years before the birth of Christ. God rested on the seventh day **(Genesis 2:1–3)**. On the eighth day of creation, God created another "man" (about 4,004 BC), one to till the ground, a farmer. This "man" (Hebrew "eth-ha adham"), He created from the dust of the ground and breathed life into him **(Genesis 2:4–7)**. From this man and his wife Eve (Hebrew for "mother of all living") is established the bloodline of Jesus and all lives eternal.

After Adam and Eve violated God's first commandment **(Genesis 2:17)**, God asked Eve what she had done. Eve replied to the Father saying Satan had beguiled her (Hebrew "nasha," to seduce utterly), and she did eat (partook) **(Genesis 3:13)**. So we see that Eve had been utterly seduced, which in most English dictionaries means to "thoroughly engage in illicit sexual intercourse." Note that there is never any mention in the Bible of Eve having "eaten an apple."

Adam knew his wife Eve, and she conceived and bore Cain **(Genesis 4:1–2)**. The Bible goes on to explain that Eve "again" (an adverb meaning "once again or continued") bore his brother Abel. What we see here is Eve has given birth to nonidentical twins by two different seeds (fathers), which is very possible of course, as any doctor will verify.

Because of Satan's seduction of Eve, God curses him and puts enmity (Hebrew "eybah," meaning hostility or hatred) between Satan and Eve and Satan's seed (Cain) and his offspring and Eve's seed, the bloodline of Jesus. God states that Eve's seed will bruise Satan's head (the complete destruction of Satan), and Satan will bruise Christ's heel (a temporary suffering of her seed) **(Genesis 3:14–15)**.

The brothers had grown and were in the field one day when Cain rose up against Abel and slew him (Hebrew "harag," meaning to smite with deadly intent, destroy, kill, murder, put to death, slay) **(Genesis 4:8)**. Mankind's first murder had been committed. Satan has sown evil into the world which is also manifested through his son Cain.

After Cain murdered his brother, God drove him from the garden of Eden where he (Cain) dwelt in the land of "Nod" (Hebrew

STUDY 3

meaning wanderer or flight) on the east of Eden **(Genesis 4:16)**. It is there that Cain met his wife, and she gave birth to their son Enoch **(Genesis 4:17)**. At this point in the Bible, Cain's genealogy is given **(Genesis 4:17–24)**.

To fully understand how the land of Nod came into existence to which Cain took flight from the garden of Eden and met his wife, we have to go to the New Testament. Peter explains that one of God's "days" is the equivalent of a thousand years to man **(2 Peter 3:8)**. God's environment is in a different dimension **(1 Corinthians 15:44–50)** than ours on earth, and time as we measure it is but a blink of an eye to our heavenly Father. This also helps us to better understand God's "days" of creation, discussed earlier, when we realize each "day" as a thousand-year period.

The first "adam" (mankind), which were all the races, had been created six thousand years (the sixth day) into God's period of creation, and the "eth-ha adham" man, to till the earth and the bloodline from which Jesus would come, was created about two thousand years afterward on the eighth day of creation. Understanding this, we now see that Nod, which was to the east of the garden, had been in existence nearly two thousand years before the creation of "eth-ha adham" and the garden of Eden, which explains how Cain's wife had been in existence for him to meet.

Adam and Eve's genealogy begins in **Genesis 4:25–32** and continues four thousand years throughout the Bible, up to the birth of Jesus in 4 BC. Note three things at this point: (1) Cain is not entered into Adam's genealogy because he is not of Adam's seed, (2) Abel has no genealogy as he was murdered before he had the opportunity to marry and have any children, and (3) Adam's genealogy begins about 3,874 BC. with the birth of their second son, Seth or Sheth (Hebrew meaning "substituted"), for Eve said, "[F]or God hath appointed me another seed instead of Abel, whom Cain slew" **(Genesis 4:25; 5:32)**.

Many generations following the garden of Eden, our heavenly Father made a covenant with Abram of "a promise land" where God will make Abram a "great nation" between the river of Egypt and the Euphrates's river **(Genesis 15:18)**. At this time, ten different tribes lived in this region, including "the Kenites" **(Genesis 15:19–21)**.

The name "Kenite" is from the Hebrew word *qeyniy* or *qiyniy*, meaning a Kenite or a member of the tribe Kajin, an oriental tribe, and Cain-Kenite. The Kenites are a tribe of peoples from the offspring of Cain, the bloodline of Satan. Do not confuse the Kenites with the "Canaanites" of the land of "Canaan." The Kenites and the Canaanites are two different tribes/races of peoples.

Around 1,491 BC, Moses fulfilled God's covenant with Abram (Abraham) regarding the promise land. Moses led the Israelites out of four hundred years of Egyptian enslavement into this land, a forty-year sojourn recorded in the Old Testament. Here again and many years later, we still find the Kenites mentioned as an inhabitant of the region **(Numbers 24:21–22)**.

The Israelites had been settled into their homeland for about five hundred years when Saul was chosen by God as their first man-king **(1 Samuel 9:15–17)**. On many occasions during this era, it is recorded that the Israelites had shown favor to the Kenites for their kindness toward them **(1 Samuel 15:1–6)**. David was emerging as a renowned warrior around 965 BC. It is recorded that he had spared the Kenites **(1 Samuel 27:8–10)** and, in fact, had actually rewarded them for their service to him **(1 Samuel 30:26–29)**. Individual Kenites have been known to follow God such as Heber and his wife Jael **(Judges 4:10–24)**. Heber lived with Moses's father-in-law, Hobar, who was a Midianite **(Numbers 10:29)**. Heber and his wife Jael had served God and were blessed by Him **(Judges 5:24)**.

Over the next nine hundred years, the Kenites, as a tribe or race of people, continued to assimilate into obscurity among the tribes of Israel and the rest of the known world through cohabitation and marriages. They had integrated into highly honored community positions with the Israelites such as scribes keeping the books **(1 Chronicles 2:55)**, teachers, as many of them could read and write, musicians, and even into their place of worship, the synagogues (churches). On one occasion, Jesus, now well into His ministry on earth, identifies the Pharisees and accompanying Jews with them as Kenites. Believing so, they told Jesus that they were of Abraham's bloodline, but Jesus corrected them to the truth that they were not but rather of their father, the devil **(John 8:39–44)**. Jesus warned

His disciples against the doctrines being taught by the Pharisees and Sadducees (priests of the synagogues) with his parable of "leavened" bread, a representation of uncleanliness, to their "leavened" or false doctrines being taught in the church **(Matthew 16:11–12)**.

Satan's mode of operation has never changed from the beginning and never will—deception, temptation, and lies. Satan very subtly and slowly works his way into our hearts and lives through our weaknesses, complacencies, fears, and ignorance until he has gained control of our very souls—if we let him.

Throughout the Bible, there is a constant theme portraying positive actions against negative actions. Good and evil, eternal life and eternal death, Christ and the antichrist, etc. The Apostle John, in his letter to the Asiatic churches, brings forth an example of opposite actions between loving one another and the hatred of Cain (of the wicked one Satan) who murdered his brother **(1 John 3:11–12)**.

In the book of **Revelation chapters 2** and **3**, Jesus describes seven churches of which He is only pleased with two—Smyrna and Philadelphia **(Revelation 2:7–11, 3:6–12)**. The common issue shared by these two churches is they were familiar with and teaching about "the synagogue of Satan, which say they (the Kenites) are Jews and are not but do lie" **(Revelation 2:9, 3:9)**. Again, Jesus identifies and warns us of the Kenites in His parable of the tares **(Matthew 13:24–30)**. Jesus explains this parable in greater detail to His disciples so there is no misunderstanding or confusion, illustrating the permeation of the children of Satan within the world we live **(Matthew 13:36–43)**.

Obviously, our understanding of the Kenites is of great importance to our Father, as the Kenites have been brought to our attention over and over throughout the Bible, deeply woven from the beginning (the garden of Eden) to the revealing of the end (Revelation). Why? To teach us that Satan's evil is brought forth from generation to generation by him and his children. Satan's deceptions, false doctrines, and lies have infiltrated all walks of life, especially in today's world arenas of education, economics, religion, and politics. Ponder these areas for a moment and look within our own country. Look at what our churches are teaching—or better still, not teaching. Look at the absence of God in our educational systems, replaced with man's philosophies and theories as "truths." Do we not see our country's economy on the brink of collapse? Every level of our political system is wrought with deceptions, lies, greed, and self-serving interests.

These are the very four dynasties used in implementing the one world system brought into play with Satan's return to earth **(Revelation chapters 13, 16, and 18)**.

As was illustrated earlier, however, not all Kenites have to be followers of their father Satan, just as all people will not be followers of Christ. God created us all and said, "It was very good" **(Genesis 1:31)**. Regardless of bloodline, national origin, race, color, or gender, when we truly repent of our sins, for God knows our hearts **(Luke 16:15)**, each of us may obtain God's forgiveness no matter who we are or what we have been **(2 Peter 3:9; John 3:16)** with the exception of one—Satan **(Ezekiel 28:18–19)**. God is the potter, the Creator of all His children **(Romans 9:18–21)**. God created all of us for His pleasure **(Revelation 4:11)**. None of us are qualified to judge anyone on God's behalf **(Matthew 7:1–5)**. We learn to love the sinner but hate the sin.

Because of our propensity to sin due to the weaknesses of our flesh bodies, we must maintain a constant vigil against evil. God has gone into great detail to teach us with example after example in his letter to us (the Bible) which guides and directs our daily lives by the power of His Holy Spirit. God has given us the ability to discern between good and evil through training **(Hebrews 5:14)** as a spiritual gift **(1 Corinthian 2:10–12)** and the Bible, which is a discerner of the right path for those that serve Him **(Malachi 3:18; Hebrews 4:12)**. God has even forewarned us of future events so that we might be prepared to stand against Satan but only in the name of Jesus are we able to do this **(Luke 10:17–20)** because we are no match against Satan on our own.

In observing the behaviors of mankind today, we often ask ourselves the question, "How can someone be so evil?" Now we know and understand the answer through the teaching of God's Word of the true principalities at work on this earth and their origin.

We are each placed in this earth age to choose who we will follow—our heavenly Father or Satan. Don't be deceived!

Religion

The word *religion* is mentioned five times in the Bible—once in the book of **Acts 26:5** and twice in the book of **Galatians 1:13–14**, as the Apostle Paul gives testimony of his earlier life as a "Pharisee" (#5330) member of the Jewish religion. The word *religion* is used twice more in the book of **James 1:18–27** where "pure religion" is defined by our heavenly Father.

By English standards, the word *religion* is defined as "beliefs, attitude, emotions, behavior, etc., constituting man's relationship with powers of the universe, deities, God, goddess or divine person."

God's definition is "[p]ure religion and undefiled before God and the Father is this, to visit the fatherless and widows in their affliction and to keep himself unspotted from the world" **(James 1:27)**.

"Man's religion" originates when he interferes with God's Word, the Bible. Man has a propensity to glorify himself centered on his own pride and personal beliefs which are passed down through religious "doctrines" (#1322), instruction, or teachings of a particular principle or tenant (list of doctrines) created from emotional behaviors, traditions, and philosophies, resulting in a theology (a body of doctrines) set forth by a particular religious group rather than, and often far from, the simplicity of God's truths as written in His Word. Some religious leaders have even gone so far as to replace Jesus Christ Himself as the head of the church, the very goal of Satan **(Ezekiel chapter 28)**.

To this end (religions created by man), God gives us His severe warnings in several places of the Bible against those who would establish such practices such as **Galatians 1:6–12**, wherein He states, "Let him be accursed (#331)," banned, excommunicated, and to the perpetrator(s) who would ultimately cause division (religious groups, denominations) and deception within *Christ's church* (**Romans 16:17–18**), God promises His final judgement against them as brought forth in **Revelation 22:16–19**. God's judgement begins at the pulpit of *His church*, the *house of God* (**1 Peter 4:17–18**).

God tells us there is only *one church—His* (**1 Corinthians 1:10–13**). God's Son, *Jesus Christ, alone is the Head of His church* and its many-membered body (**Colossians 1:18**).

God tells us there is only *one Bible* (**Galatians 1:6–9**). All scripture is given by inspiration of God and is profitable (advantageous for gain) for doctrine, for reproof (evidence, proof), for correction (instruction in righteousness) that the man of God may be perfect and thoroughly furnished (prepared) unto all good works (**2 Timothy 3:16–17**).

Christianity is not a religion, rather a way of living life with our Father, His Son Jesus Christ, and His Holy Spirit as our teachers through His Word. It is the letter He wrote to us—for us, His children. Jesus has told us *all* things (**Mark 13: 28**) from the very beginning of God's story—His story (history) and into the future (prophecy). From the very beginning was the Word, the Word was with God and the Word was God and the Word became flesh and dwelt among us (**John 1:1, 14**).

Early on in Christ's ministry, believers were first known as followers of "the Way" (a path or road) as directed by Jesus's teachings concerning man's pathway to salvation and God's eternal kingdom. Shortly after Christ's resurrection, groups of His followers began to miraculously increase as His truths were beginning to be revealed to them by the Holy Spirit through the continued teaching of Christ's message by the apostles. Those who first trusted and believed after they heard the word of truth, the gospel (good news) of salvation, were sealed with the Holy Spirit of promise (**Ephesians 1:12–14**). At this time, the beginning of Christ's church had formed and began to spread and grow in great numbers throughout the world (**Ephesians 1:21–23**). Early believers first came to be known as "Christians" (Christ-man) at the church in Antioch as recorded in the Bible during the reign of the Roman emperor Claudius Caesar (**Acts 11:26–27**), circa AD 33 to 37.

STUDY 4

Christ's church is formed by a many-membered body of believers constituting Christ's body. No one person is greater than another, each different, with individual offices of responsibility (gifts), yet one body in Christ **(Romans 12:3–5)**. Again, *Jesus Christ is the Head of the body, the church* **(Colossians 1:18)**. As the many-membered body of believers in Him—His church—and with Jesus Christ as our High Priest over the house of God, it is through His blood sacrificed on the cross for our sins that we, as individual children of God, are able to commune directly with our Father **(Hebrews 10:12–22)**.

Because of our Father's faithful promise of eternal life, it is the duty of Christians to hold fast our profession of faith in Him without wavering, supporting one another with love and good works, promoting opportunities to assemble ourselves together as the body of Christ's church in the *house of the Lord* **(Hebrews 10:23–25)**. In earlier times and even now occasionally, the "house" of the Lord was a person's home where friends, neighbors, relatives, and other Christians would gather to worship: "For where two or three are gathered together in My name, there am I in the midst of them" **(Matthew 18:20)**. "Church" (#1577) is not a building but a community of members assembled to worship God.

We assemble ourselves as Christians to "worship" (#7812/4352), to pay homage, adorn, and revere God in the name of Jesus Christ by the power of The Holy Spirit, to seek Him and understand His will from His Word by reading His Word "[t]hat we might know the things that are freely given to us by God. Which things also we speak not in the words which mans' wisdom teacheth, but which the Holy Spirit teacheth comparing spiritual things with spiritual" **(1 Corinthians 2:12–13)**.

> **But the Comforter, which is the Holy Spirit, whom the Father will send in My name, He shall teach you all things, and bring all things to your remembrance what so ever I have said to you. (John 4:26)**

From the earliest time of God's written Word, we see that Moses taught by reading the manuscripts (Bible) of the Old Testament aloud at the assembly of His people **(Exodus 24:7)**. In like manner, Jesus Christ "preached" (#2097/2606, meaning to declare, show, proclaim, teach) in the synagogues (the Jewish meeting place of worship and instruction), reading aloud to the assembly from the Old Testament **(Luke 4:14–20)** while continually teaching aloud His living testimony of the gospel (good news) of God's kingdom to come among His disciples and gathered crowds **(Matthew 4:23)**.

As seen by these examples, we too need to assemble ourselves in love for our heavenly Father in the name of Jesus Christ by the power of the Holy Spirit, to pursue Him and His wisdom in understanding His will through His truths as simply written in His Word.

With the knowledge of God's Truth, we will be prepared to recognize any injection of man's traditions, doctrines, or theologies established from picking and choosing what some may or may not want to believe or the insertion of man's philosophies based on man's perceived intellect rather than God's Word **(Mark 7:5–13)**. Such obstructions developed over centuries underscore the real need for teachers to provide instruction with understanding of the truth by making clear the very words of the Bible from the original language(s), if necessary, beginning with chapter one, verse one, continuing cover to cover, chapter by chapter, and verse by verse. Each believer fulfilling the body of Christ's church has been given "spiritual gifts" as God has chosen, including the gift of "discernment," the ability to know truth from lies **(1 Corinthians 12:1–12)**. Even God's new covenant with man included the instilling of His laws in our minds and heart **(Hebrews 8:10),** thus man instinctively knows the difference between right and wrong.

Church is not a building, religious denomination, or theology. God intended there to be *only one church—His*. "Built upon the foundation of the Apostles [New Testament] and the prophets [Old Testament] with Jesus Christ Himself being the cornerstone" **(Ephesians 2:20)**.

STUDY 4

The Apostle Paul, speaking at the church of Corinth, said,

> **Now I beseech [#3870, to exhort, call for, desire] you brethren, by the name of our Lord Jesus Christ, that ye all speak the same thing and that there be no divisions [#1370, dissention; #4978, split; #4977, sever, break] among you, but that ye be perfectly joined together in the same mind and in the same judgement" (1 Corinthians 1:10–13).**

God warns us in **Romans 16:17–18** against denominationalism, a disposition to divide into or form denominations or religious groups ("religions") as a result of man's philosophies, doctrines, and traditions (see also **Colossians chapter 2 and Acts chapter 17**). God makes known to believers whether or not we are hearing man's doctrine rather than that of God's doctrines (**John 7:14–18**) and warns us not to become carried away by them knowing that Jesus is the same yesterday, today, and forever (**Hebrews 13:8–9**).

Jesus instructs us to preach the gospel (**Mark 1:14–15**) to the whole world (**Mark 16:15**), only the Word (**2 Timothy 4:1–4**), the whole Word (**Ephesians 2:20**), and the truth (**Ephesians 4:14–15**).

As previously mentioned, God's judgement of man begins with the *house of God*, the very pulpit and members of *His church*, and our obedience to *His gospel* (**1 Peter 4:17**). For this reason, as Christians, we need to pray for our teachers (**Ephesians 6:18–20**), that only God's Word is taught and God's truth is thoroughly understood by all hearing it.

Our heavenly Father gives us a stern warning against those of us who choose not to believe His truths and continue down the path of unrighteousness: "And for this cause God shall send them strong delusion, that they should believe a lie" (**2 Thessalonians 2:9–12**). Ultimately, each of us as individuals, without any assistance from a preacher, pastor, priest, rabbi, reverend, bishop, etc., will stand alone before God and be held responsible for our own actions or inactions as we knowingly choose them. You might say, "Well, I didn't know," and Father might ask, "Didn't you read the letter I sent you?" What will you answer?

Right from wrong, good from evil, truth from lie—Satan will attempt to keep us from the Bible and God's truths just as he attempted to deceive Jesus **(Luke 4:1–13)**, but knowing the Bible will keep us from Satan and his lies.

What church do we choose, and how do we make the right choice? First, we pray to our Father in the name of Jesus Christ, by the power of the Holy Spirit for His guidance **(John 16:13–14).**

If you are currently attending or looking to attend a church which is teaching doctrine that you think may not be in alignment with God's Word, study the issue yourself from God's Word then discern with knowledge from rightly dividing the scripture **(2 Timothy 2:15–16).** Take no man's word without checking it yourself. Respectfully, you might ask an intelligent question of the teacher and ask to be shown from the Bible that you may better understand by clarifying the position without argument as it serves no purpose **(2 Timothy 2:23–26; Titus 3:9; James 3:1–2).** Perhaps God's will has placed you in that position for His purpose to teach others or maybe it's time to search for another church. Again, through prayer, ask our Father for His Holy Spirit to lead, guide, and direct you as to His will.

As you search for a church that pleases God in their teaching, we first know that God's Word is to be taught and only His truths.

We know that the gospel of Jesus Christ and His message of God's eternal kingdom and our salvation is of utmost importance (the key of David).

We can make a list from the Bible of other important lessons, which should be taught within every one of God's assembled houses of worship beginning with instructions found in the Book of **Titus**.

The book of **Revelation chapters 2 and 3** lists Jesus's discussions with the seven churches—likes and dislikes. Of these seven churches, He is pleased with only two of them—Smyrna **(Revelation 2:8–11)** and Philadelphia **(Revelation 3:7–13)**. What sets themselves apart from the other churches is these two churches taught about the "Kenites" (#7017/7014, meaning children of Cain, offspring of Satan), "those who say they are Jews and are not, but are of the synagogue of Satan" as Jesus taught **(John 8:39–44)**, and "God's mystery" spoken of since the beginning **(Matthew 13:35–51).**

Are the details of the book of **Revelation** taught, such as the seven trumps, vials, and seals **(Revelation chapters 6 through 17)** also found summarized in **Matthew chapter 24, Mark chapter 13, Luke chapter 21**? Do they teach the fact that Satan (666) returns to this earth first in his period of tribulation (sixth trump, sixth vial, sixth seal) as the antichrist "and the whole world will be deceived" prior to the return of Jesus Christ who returns on the seventh trump (six before seven) or do they teach "man's rapture theory" versus God's Word?

The list is endless; parable of the fig tree, God's law and grace, personal access to Our heavenly Father, three earth and heaven ages, God's elect, and so, so much more which literally opens the mind by clearing the fog to understanding.

In essence, read and study the Holy Bible in its entirety, chapter by chapter, and verse by verse. Wisdom, detailed in the book of **Proverbs chapter 8**, begins with knowing and understanding God's Word.

Note: The numbers found in parenthesis (#0000) following certain words in this study are the word number keys referencing either the Hebrew/Chaldee or Greek language dictionaries from the *Strong's Exhaustive Concordance of The Bible*.

The Rapture Theory versus God's Word, the Bible

Nowhere in the Bible does our Father speak of a pre- or post-tribulation "rapture" of His children (Christians) in the end times. In fact, God is against those that would teach a "flyaway" (rapture) to save their souls **(Ezekiel 13:18–23)**. This letter is *not* an in-depth study, but merely *an overview* of this subject with recommendations that you take time to understand and do your own research and study of God's letter to us, the Bible.

The "rapture theory" has been evangelicalism's most popular interpretation of the future. This escapist belief has been successfully employed by many pulpits, seminaries, and even Hollywood, since 1830. Many times I, as many others, have been told that it wasn't necessary to understand the book of **Revelation** because as a Christian, indoctrinated in a pre- or post-tribulation view of Christ's second coming, I wouldn't be here on earth anyway. As a Christian, I will be "raptured" in the clouds with Christ before Satan's return, and only nonbelievers will be "left behind." If this is the case, why would the books of **Mark, Matthew, Luke, Revelation**, and others even be relevant? Why would Jesus teach and the apostles preach the events of both Satan's and Christ's periods of tribulation? The answer is so that we, "the generation of the fig tree" **(Jeremiah chapter 24),** will understand our role and responsibility as Christians during these times, which is to "just plant the seed" and "do God's commandments" **(Revelation 22:10–15)**. We must remain faithful to our

Father, placing our trust in Him and His promises, knowing that we, as Christians, have nothing to fear **(Revelation 2:10, 7:1, 9:4, 21:4)**!

The origin or the "rapture theory" started in 1830, traced back to visions expressed by Ms. Margaret Macdonald of Port Glasgow, Scotland, following an eighteen-month illness she had experienced. She noticed that something happens after the **Matthew 24:40** "taken" and after **2 Thessalonians 2:7** "taken."

These verses read:

> **Then shall two be in the field; the one shall be taken, and the other left. (Matthew 24:40)**
>
> **For the mystery of iniquity doth already work; only he who now letteth will let, until he be taken out of the way. (2 Thessalonians 2:7)**

Putting the two passages together, she reasoned that only after the "rapture," when some would be left on earth would the antichrist then be revealed. Somehow, she reasons **Matthew's** "taking away" with **2 Thessalonians'** "taking out of the way" after Christ's return, introducing escapism, when no one in eighteen centuries preceding her had ever tied these two "takens" together before.

Author David MacPherson spent over twenty-five years researching, investigating, and documenting this "mother of all revisionisms" in his book entitled *The Rapture Plot* (Artisan Publishers, 1994, 2000, ISBN 0-934666-85-7), a required read for an in-depth understanding of how this very misleading lie catches on just prior to the end times. Curious, isn't it? We know why—"for many will be deceived." As we know, Satan is the great deceiver, a biblical lawyer. He first deceived Adam and Eve and even attempted to deceive Jesus during His forty days in the wilderness. Jesus's defense, of course, was knowing the Word, and we must too.

Matthew 24:40 refers to Satan's arrival with two working— one leaves the field to work for and worship Satan, unknowingly believing he is Christ **(Revelation 13:11–18)**, and the other is left in the field standing firm, continuing God's work as a continuing testimony against Satan.

First, we have to understand that we have two bodies—the flesh body and the spiritual body **(1 Corinthians 15:35–49)**. When our flesh bodies die or "sleep," as used interchangeably with the word *die*, our spiritual body doesn't lie in a hole in the ground but is instantly returned to the Father who created it **(Ecclesiastes 12:6–7)**. Flesh and blood cannot enter heaven because heaven is of a different dimension **(1 Corinthians 15:50)**. If we believe Jesus died for our sins and rose again defeating death, then we must also believe that we too will rise on the death of our flesh bodies. Those of us here at the sounding of the seventh trump when Christ returns will *all* (believers and non-believers) be changed to our spiritual or incorruptible bodies "in the twinkling of an eye" **(1 Corinthians 15:51–58)**. Note: some souls will remain corruptible (liable to die), however, until God's judgement after the millennium. Another great study for another time!

As believers **(John 3:16)**, we should be unafraid of the physical death **(2 Corinthians 5:6–8)** or to stand before the judgement of God if, with repentant hearts, we ask for forgiveness of our sins committed while in these flesh bodies. This is *the* matter of eternal life or eternal death of our spiritual souls and bodies for which Jesus died on the cross, for us.

The Apostle Paul explains this in **1 Thessalonians 4:13–18**, but it is often misunderstood. We have to remember to follow the subject of the writing which is Paul explaining as to "where the dead [those asleep] are." In **Verse 16** when he speaks of "the dead in Christ shall rise first," it is because they (the dead) have already risen, so of course they have risen first. Paul also uses Greek colloquialism of the day with the word *cloud* in **Verse 17**, which refers to "a gathering" or "group" like a cloud of locusts or something, not a cloud in the sky. And in the same verse, he uses the word *air*, which when properly translated from the Greek means "spirit," not air or oxygen we breathe. This is where a good *Strong's Concordance* plays a valuable role toward "rightly dividing" God's Word.

In **2 Thessalonians chapter 2**, Paul further explains our "gathering together unto Him" but that Satan, the false Christ **(Isaiah**

14:13–16), must come first, at the sixth trump. We are not only gathered to Jesus but also His army **(Revelation chapter 19)**. And where does His army that accompanies Him come from? Of those saints that are already in paradise with Him. Jesus gives us an example of paradise and the gulf between two people having arrived there after their deaths **(Luke 16:19–31)**.

The book of **Revelation**—the revealing, or in Greek translation, "uncovering/unveiling"—must be read, taught, and understood as God reveals in detail just how things will come about during the two tribulation periods (Satan's and Christ's). He explains the seven seals, seven trumps, seven vials, warnings to the seven churches, the three woes, one-world order, four dynasties (education, political, economic, religion), the new heaven and earth, and so much more. Satan and his followers are cast down to earth at the sixth trump **(Revelation 6:11–17** "the antichrist" and further described in **Revelation 12:7–10)**. Jesus returns to earth at the seventh Trump **(Revelation 11:15)** with His armies from heaven to make war against Satan and his followers described in **Revelation 19:11–21**. *Note*: **Revelation 13:18** (sixth seal, sixth trump, sixth vial, all to do with Satan, "666"), again, a study for another time. Satan returns before Jesus Christ (six comes before seven) as the antichrist ("anti" in Greek translated as "instead of"), as is warned and taught by Jesus, the prophets, and apostles over and over. Michael then comes down from heaven (to the earth) and lays hold on the devil until the end of the millennium **(Revelation 20:1)**. At the end of the thousand-year period (millennium), a time of teaching, Satan is cast into the lake of fire forever and ever **(Revelation 20:7–10)**. More on life in the millennium can be found in the book of **Ezekiel chapters 40 through 48**. The new heaven and new earth happen here, on this earth **(Revelation chapter 21)**. The New Jerusalem comes to earth from heaven **(Revelation 21:1)**. And God Himself is here (on the new earth) to be with us and live with us (wherever God is, heaven is) for eternity **(Revelation 21:3)**.

As Christians, the Lord expects us to be strong, stand as men and women of God, to be faithful to Him, for our fight isn't with flesh but of principalities, the devil, and spiritual wickedness in high places. We are expected to be soldiers for Christ taking on the whole armor of God, that we may be able to withstand the evil day of Satan's return without worry **(Ephesians 6:10–17)**.

Oh, and a word of encouragement in reading the book of **Revelation** with all the "symbolisms" such as beasts, horns, locust army, sea, etc.—God actually explains these terms if you don't stop there and read on. Sometimes however, they are found explained in Old Testament prophecies too.

God expects us to read His letter to us, the Bible, to seal His Word "in our foreheads" (the seven seals), to protect and save us, teach us how to live in these flesh bodies while here on earth, understand history, including the previous earth and heaven age, the purpose of this earth and heaven age, and the future earth and heaven age to come. The three earth and heaven ages, another wonderful study in itself.

Jesus's first warning to us when His disciples asked Him about the end times was "Don't be deceived" **(Luke 21:8; Matthew 24:4; Mark 13:5)**. "Many shall come in My name, saying I am Christ [i.e., Christian preachers, etc.] and shall deceive many" **(Mark 13:6)**. In the book of **Mark chapter 13**, Jesus provides an overview of the events of the end times, the seven trumps. Satan's period of tribulation occurs first **(Mark 13:8–23)**, followed by Christ's period of tribulation **(Mark 13:24–37)**, again with severe warnings to the church(s) against false teachings. **Matthew chapter 24 and Luke chapter 21** give witness to this account as well.

The Birth of Jesus Christ (and Christmas)

Prophecy

Our heavenly Father provided us with the first clue of the coming of His Son and Savior, Jesus Christ, four thousand years in advance of His arrival—the first prophesy of the Bible **(Genesis 3:15)**. There continues other prophecies of Jesus throughout the Old Testament as well.

A biblical prophecy is a commandment from God telling us in advance of certain events as to how they will transpire in accordance with His plans—His will. Prophecies are not of men but of the Holy Spirit of God **(1 Peter 1:20–21)**. Prophecies are meant to prepare, warn, and instruct us as to future events that we might believe and trust in Him, our God and heavenly Father. He has told us all things **(Mark 13:23)**.

Approximately six hundred fifty years before His birth, God prophesied in the Old Testament that His Son's name will be "Immanuel" **(Isaiah 7:14)**. Immanuel is a Hebrew name (#6005) meaning "God with us." Similarly, God prophesied an outline of Jesus's life on earth recorded in **Isaiah chapter 53**.

The Good News

The four books of **Matthew, Mark, Luke, and John** are collectively referred to as the Gospels. They are all found in the beginning of the New Testament. They provide four individual and distinct reported accounts of Jesus resulting in one perfect whole. The Gospels bring to life His conception, birth, ministry, crucifixion, death on earth, to His triumphant resurrection, and purpose providing man's salvation and eternal life. The word *gospel* is Greek (#2098) meaning "good news."

This study focuses on the Gospel according to Luke as presented by the Holy Spirit of God without the interference of the myths and traditions of man. The book of **Luke** chronologically records and documents the history, fulfillment of prophecy, eye witness accounts, and dates of events surrounding Jesus's birth and first year(s) of His life as written in God's Word, the Bible.

Luke, an educated physician at the time of Jesus's ministry **(Colossians 4:14)**, opens his gospel by standing in agreement with other Christians that a need existed to establish in writing, the facts relative to the birth of Jesus **(Luke 1:1–4)**.

World History

Luke begins setting up the period of Jesus's birth with a timeline of historical facts by introducing the world leaders of the era. He begins with King Herod who ruled over Judah at this time **(Luke 1:5)**. King Herod was declared king of Judah by the Romans in 39 BC and died sometime between 3 BC and 2 BC. Mentioned later in his text is Cesar Augustus (Octavius) **(Luke 2:1)**. Augustus was the emperor of Rome beginning in 31 BC and died on August 19, AD 14. Additionally, Luke documents that a man named Cyrenius (Publius Sulpicius Quirinus) was governor of Syria. This is important historically because he governed at the same time Augustus decreed "that the whole world should be taxed" **(Luke 2:2)**. Cyrenius ruled from 4 BC to 1 BC, narrowing our focus within these three years.

Genealogy

The genealogy of Jesus Christ ("Son of Man") is also very important. This historical documentation provides the direct route of His ancestry beginning four thousand years earlier from Adam and

STUDY 6

Eve, umbilical cord to umbilical cord, all the way to Mary's father, Heldi of the tribe of Judah, the king line of David of Israel **(Luke 3:23–38)**.

Joseph's ancestry, also of the king line of David, is recorded in the book of **Matthew 1:1–16**. Note in **verse 16** that Joseph's genealogy does not record him as having "begat" (fathered) Jesus because Jesus is "the only begotten Son of God," through His Holy Spirit **(Matthew 1:18)**. Joseph is Jesus's stepfather as declared by the angel of the Lord **(Matthew 1:18–25)**.

Mary's ancestry brings together the king line of the tribe of Judah via her father and the priest line of the tribe of Levi via her mother who was a Levite. This very important issue is established by Luke with the introduction of Mary's cousin, Elisabeth **(Luke 1:38)**, who is "of the daughters of Aaron," wife of the Levite priest Zacharias of the Course of Abia **(Luke 1:5)**, and parents of John the Baptist **(Luke 1:13)**. For Mary and Elisabeth to have been cousins, Mary's mother and Elisabeth's mother had to have been sisters, both of the tribe of Levi.

Only direct decedents of Moses's brother Aaron could be priests to Israel **(Exodus 28:1)**. All priests are Levites, but not all Levites are priests, and only another Levite woman (daughter of Aaron) could marry a Levitical priest. Mary's mother married outside her tribe of Levi into the tribe of Judah when she married Mary's father Heldi, while her sister (Elisabeth's mother) married within their tribe of Levi as did her daughter Elisabeth who eventually married Zacharias, priest of the Course of Abia.

The significance of this connection of merging bloodlines between the king line from the tribe of Judah (Mary's father) and the priest line from the tribe of Levi (Mary's mother) culminates the fulfillment of Jesus's titles as "King of Kings" **(1 Timothy 6:15)**, "Priest of High" **(Hebrew 8:40)**, "Prophet of the Highest" **(Luke 1:76)**, "the Perfect Man, the Son of God" **(John 1:34),** and the fulfillment of God's prophecy of His new covenant (Jesus) with His people, the house of Israel and the house of Judah **(Jeremiah 31:31)**.

BIBLE STUDIES 102

The Hebrew Calendar

The civil year of the Hebrew calendar begins on October 6 (twenty-second day of Tisri) following the eighth and last day of the Feast of the Tabernacle, which starts on September 29 (fifteenth Tisri) and lasts seven days until the end of their civil year (October 6).

The Course of Abia

Knowing that Elisabeth's husband Zacharias is the priest of the Course of Abia allows the application of precise dates to the timeline of Jesus's birth.

Each of twenty-four priests were assigned a particular period of duty serving twice each year called a "course" in which they were responsible for the ministering functions of the temple of God as established in **1 Chronicles 24:7–19**. Each of these courses is titled from the names of the original priests that served in these positions, and the dates of each also remained as first assigned by lot from the beginning. Therefore, we know that the eighth Course of Abia is ministered for the first time in the Hebrew calendar between the twelfth through the eighteenth (Sabbath to Sabbath) of the Hebrew month of Chislen (December 6 through the 12). The second time of the year that the Course of Abia is ministered is between the twelfth through the eighteenth of the Hebrew month of Sivan (June 13 through the 19). From these dates, in conjunction with other information presented by Luke, we will see that the Priest Zacharias was ministering the Course of Abia for the second time that year between the dates of June 13 to 19 (Sabbath to Sabbath) in the year 5 BC.

John's Conception

The birth of John (the Baptist) to Zacharias and Elisabeth holds overwhelming importance for the world whose purpose is to "make ready a people prepared for the Lord" **(Luke 1:17)**. John is Jesus's cousin, and the two were conceived and born six months apart. The documenting of important events surrounding John's birth establishes a base line of dates to work from essential to our understanding of God's truths relative to the birthdate of His Son Jesus.

The two dates of the Course of Abia which was ministered by the priest Zacharias are December 6 to 12 and again in June 13 19. Zacharias was ministering his tasks at the temple of the Lord in Jerusalem when the angel of the Lord (Gabriel) spoke to him telling him of the birth of John and that his son will be filled with the Holy Spirit even while in Elisabeth's womb **(Luke 1:8–15)**.

After Zacharias had completed his ministration, he went home **(Luke 1:23)**. The end of his ministration is June 19, a Saturday. Following the Course of Abia (Sivan 12 to 18), the next day would have been June 20, the Sabbath (Sivan 19). Zacharias would not have been allowed to travel on the Sabbath so he wouldn't have physically departed until the following day, Monday, the twenty-first. Being "well stricken in years" **(Luke 1:7)** as a senior citizen, it is likely to have taken him two or three days to travel the thirty miles from Jerusalem to his home (although not named may have been Juttah) in the hill country of Judah **(Luke 1:39–40)**, placing his arrival on the twenty-third or twenty-fourth of June (twenty-third of Sivan).

Elisabeth conceived during this time and hid herself for five months **(Luke 1:24)**. From the date in which Zacharias had returned home (June 23 or 24) plus the five months in which Elisabeth hid herself, we have arrived at the date of November 24, 5 BC.

Mary's Conception

Scripture now changes the subject to the arrival of the angel Gabriel at Mary's home in Nazareth to explain to Mary that she will conceive a child by the Holy Spirit whose name is Jesus, who "shall be called the Son of God" **(Luke 1:26–35)**. Gabriel also tells Mary that her cousin Elisabeth is with child and is in her sixth month of pregnancy **(Luke 1:36)**. From the date of the five months stated above (November 24), forward to Elisabeth's sixth month, we arrive at the date of December 25 (first Tebeth), the date of Mary's conception—*not* the birth of Jesus.

BIBLE STUDIES 102

The Birth of John

Mary arose and departed for Elisabeth's house in the hill country of Judah **(Luke 1:39–40)**. When Elisabeth heard Mary entering her house, the babe (John) leaped in her womb, and Elisabeth was filled with the Holy Spirit. In a loud voice, she blessed Mary and the fruit in her womb **(Luke 1:41–44)**.

Stop a moment to contemplate what is written here in God's Word. Our heavenly Father has just told us that upon Mary's *conception*, the life and soul within her were recognized as alive and living by the Holy Spirit of God, illustrating that the life of a human being begins at the moment of conception.

Mary stayed with her cousin Elisabeth for three months and then returned to her own home in Nazareth **(Luke 1:56)**. Elisabeth's pregnancy has reached full term (nine months) at this time, giving birth to their son John **(Luke 1:57–60)**. From Mary's conception on December 25 (Elisabeth's sixth month), plus three months until John's birth, brings us to the approximate dates of March 28 to 29, 4 BC (fourth to seventh of the Hebrew month of Nisan). Eight days after his birth, as was customary of all Hebrew males by law **(Genesis 17:12)**, John was brought by his parents to the tabernacle of God and circumcised **(Luke 1:59)**. This dedication of their child to the Lord would have occurred at the start of the celebration of the High Sabbath Feast of Passover, on or about April 5 or 6 in the year 4 BC. Historically, the Feast of Passover commences annually on the fifteenth day following the spring equinox of March 21 to 22.

Historical Event

Our next recorded interval of time begins in **Luke chapter 2** with the declaration from Roman emperor Caesar Augustus "that all the world should be taxed" requiring registration or enrollment. This order of taxing was issued while Cyrenius was governor of Syria **(Luke 2:1–2)**. The announcement required everyone to return unto their city of birth to be taxed **(Luke 2:3)**. This was the first taxing by the Roman Empire; a second taxation is recorded in **Acts 5:37**.

STUDY 6

Caesar Augustus, in an attempt to keep the taxation process as calm as possible, wisely waited until after the time of harvest as a matter of practicality. The ideal time for the administration of his taxation would be when most of the people were already gathered at one location in Jerusalem celebrating the Sabbath of the Fall Festival of Tabernacle, which begins each year after the fall equinox of September 21 to 22. Additionally, the timing of the taxation during the festival would require the least amount of additional travel necessary for the population prior to winter.

The Birth of Jesus

Joseph and Mary now married, and she, near full term, departed from their home in Nazareth traveling by donkey about sixty-five to seventy miles into Judaea and the city of Bethlehem (about five miles south of Jerusalem). It is here that Joseph was to be registered and taxed as he was from Bethlehem, the house and lineage of David **(Luke 2:4–5)**.

While in Bethlehem, Mary gave birth to Jesus in a manger or stable **(Luke 2:7–7)**. There were no vacancies at any of the area inns as it was also the first day of the Feast of Tabernacles taking place at the temple in Jerusalem beginning the fifteenth of Tisri or Ethanim (September 29, 4 BC). This was the annual celebration of thanksgiving to God for harvests or "ingatherings" from the fields celebrated by Israel during the fall season of each year **(Exodus 23:16)**. With the fall festival underway and the edict of taxing taking place simultaneously, the entire area surrounding Jerusalem is overcrowded with a large number of visitors.

Eyewitnesses

There were shepherds still in the fields pasturing their sheep throughout the countryside of Bethlehem, attesting to the logic that it was not yet the winter season, as there would be no grazing of animals in the fields during winter months, such as December **(Luke 2:8)**. These are also the same fields and countryside where King David shepherded his father's sheep as a boy approximately eleven hundred years earlier **(1 Samuel 16:4, 11)**. It is in these fields that the angel of the Lord and a host of other angels appeared before a band of shepherds and announced the birth of Jesus, a Savior which is Christ the Lord, had just occurred in a manger in Bethlehem **(Luke 2:9–15)**.

After the angels had returned to heaven, the shepherds (total number unknown) immediately went to Bethlehem and searched until they found Joseph, Mary, and Jesus in the manger just as they were told by the angel of the Lord **(Luke 2:12)**. They recited the things they were told by the angel to everyone present while Mary quietly reflected on all the miracles that were taking place in her life, that day, and those of her Son's future **(Luke 2:9–15)**. The shepherds departed from them and returned to their flocks glorifying and praising God **(Luke 2:20)**.

On the eighth day after Jesus's birth, the last day of the fall festival on October 6 (twenty-second of Tisri or Ethanim), He was circumcised in accordance with the law and is named Jesus, just as the Archangel Gabriel had instructed Mary. After Mary's purification period of forty days following the birth of a male in accordance with the Law of Moses **(Leviticus 12:1–4)**, she and Joseph brought Jesus to the temple of God in Jerusalem and dedicated Him, their firstborn, to the Lord God of Israel in obedience to His command **(Exodus 13:1–2)**.

Before leaving the temple, Jesus had received additional blessing from a man named Simeon, fulfilling the prophecy of **Isaiah 9:2** and a prophetess (preacher) named Anna who gave her thanks to the Lord for sending Jesus to redeem all those looking for His salvation. Afterward, Mary, Joseph, and their Son Jesus, now about six weeks old, returned to their home in Nazareth **(Luke 2:25–39)**. We've now arrived at a date on or about November 9, 4 BC.

A short while later, there arrived in Jerusalem wise men (Greek #3097, meaning "magos," oriental scientist), from the East, the total number of which is not stated. They addressed Herod the king and innocently inquired of him as to the whereabouts of the King of Jews. They explained that they had been following a star from the East which led them there in the hope of worshiping Him.

STUDY 6

"Herod the king" was ruler over Judah at this time. He is so identified in **Matthew chapter 2** as to distinguish him from any of his sons of four different wives. Some of the other "Herods" will play their own roles in scripture and history. The utilization of a father's name, as in Herod, was customary of the period.

Herod the king gathered his sources and asked them if they had ever heard where this Christ had been born. They told him that the town was Bethlehem of Judea, as was written by the prophets (examples in **Zechariah 9:9** and **Micah 5:2**). Herod the king passed along this information to the wise men and asked that they report back to him after they found the young child **(Matthew 2:1–9)**.

The Greek word for *child* as used here is "paidion" (#3813), meaning infant or half-grown little child. The Greek word used for "babe" (baby) is *brephos* (#1025) meaning an embryo or newly born babe. From the use of the word *paidion* for young child in **Matthew 2:8**, we know some time has passed since Jesus's birth when the shepherds had first worshipped Him as a newly born babe (brephos) in the manger at Bethlehem.

When the wise men departed from Herod, the star they had been following again appeared before them, much to their surprise, indicating a miraculous or divine act rather than an astronomical phenomenon. The star continued to lead them to Jesus's house, not manger, which was in Nazareth, not Bethlehem, some sixty-five to seventy miles away. Here they found Mary and Jesus and worshipped Him presenting three gifts (gold, frankincense, and myrrh). There is nothing stated concerning the number of wise men, only the number of gifts presented **(Matthew 2:9–11)**.

God had warned the wise men in a dream not to return to Herod as he had asked so when they left Nazareth they took another route home. After they left, the angel of the Lord came to Joseph and warned him of Herod's intent to kill Jesus and told him to take Jesus and Mary into Egypt for their safety until He contacted him again after Herod the king was dead **(Matthew 2:12–15)**. Here we see another of Gods prophecies fulfilled: "Out of Egypt have I called My Son" **(Hosea 11:1)**.

Herod the king was furious when the wise men did not return to him and in his wrath ordered all the male children two years and under living in Bethlehem and surrounding area to be killed **(Matthew 2:16)**.

Jesus Returns Home

At this juncture in Jesus's life, we are able to reasonably calculate that He is a toddler between one and a half to two years of age from the information Herod the king had obtained from the wise men and the king's reasoning directing all the male children under the age of two be killed and the historical fact that Herod the king died between 3 BC and 2 BC.

After Herod the king's death, the angel of the Lord came to Joseph in a dream and told him it was safe for him and his family to return to Israel. When they had returned, Joseph discovered that one of Herod's sons (Archelaus) had assumed the office of his father, which concerned Joseph but, trusting in God, did return to Nazareth **(Matthew 2:19–23)**.

End of Story

No further information is recorded in scripture of Jesus's infancy beyond this point, but we do know that He grew strong in spirit, was filled with wisdom, and God's love was upon Him. With this statement, God's story, the "His-story" of His Son's birth, ends in **Luke 2:40**. The years of Jesus's youth are not visited in the Bible until He is twelve years old **(Luke 2:42)**.

Traditions Involving the Celebration of Christmas

The Celebration of Jesus's Conception on December 25

The Apostolic (Christian) church during the time of Christ and after was fully aware of the actual dates of His conception, birth, and crucifixion. These peoples and early Christians were witnesses to fulfilled prophecies, teachings of the apostles, and many with personal experiences as witnesses of Christ's own ministry. Such evidence is alluded to many times in scripture such as, "The Word became flesh" **(John 1:14)**, "That which is conceived in her by the Holy Spirit" **(Matthew 1:18–20)**, the recording of events in the **book of Luke** as studied, and more.

Contemplate four thousand years of anticipation of the arrival of the Messiah (God's Savior), which had endlessly grown in the hearts of believers to a point of feverish desire, hope, and expectation. This flood of contained emotions could only have exploded into a crescendo of unparalleled happiness and joyous momentum that words couldn't describe upon His miraculous advent on earth! The celebration of His arrival wouldn't wait past the inaugural ceremony of His conception on December 25, 5 BC. Just as today, over two thousand years later, Christians await His second coming, and it will transpire as prophesized by God just as His first coming did.

The actual birth of Jesus on September 29, 4 BC took place in conjunction with the beginning of the Hebrew Feast of the Tabernacle with His circumcision eight days later at the close of the festival on October 6, 4 BC. The spiritual implication shows us God's perfect timing of Jesus's birth during the Feast of the Tabernacle as God's celebration of the harvest (salvation) of His children through His Savior and Son, Jesus Christ. However, as these two events shared the same dates of this fifteen-hundred-year-old annual celebration, man's complacency, ignorance of truth through lack of knowledge, and disbelief allowed the facts surrounding His actual birth to slide into obscurity over the next two thousand years. The date of December 25, however, has stood alone in time against all generations to commemorate the astounding event, the miracle of the instant God came down from heaven, through the womb, to become flesh and dwell among men **(John 10:30, 13:7–10)**. Not surprisingly, this date has remained endlessly celebrated throughout the world unto this very day and will be forever. Sadly however, our generation is also allowing the purpose of His celebration to slide into obscurity today as our failure to teach God's truths to the next generation takes hold allowing continued complacency, ignorance, and evil to grow exponentially.

As an example, it wasn't too many years ago that in the United States, a limited number of individual presidents' birthdays were celebrated each year. Today, however, they are combined into a single celebration called "President's Day." Do you remember which presidential birthdays were celebrated individually? If you've never been taught, don't care, or don't believe, you have no idea.

The Exchange of Gifts

God presented us with His greatest gift possible; His new covenant (promise) made possible through the sacrifice of His own Son Immanuel (God with us), Jesus (God's Savior), the Christ (the Anointed One), that upon repentance of our sins and belief on Him, we may have eternal life **(John 3:16)**.

All God wants from us in return is our love for Him and our knowledge of Him **(Hosea 6:6)**. We show our love to Him by obeying His commandments and knowledge of Him by reading His letter He wrote to us, the Bible. There is no greater gift we could possibly pass on to our children.

The Evergreen Tree

Some are concerned that the traditionally decorated Christmas tree used during the celebration of Christ's conception (December 25) is contrary to God's Word based on **Jeremiah 10:3–4** of the Old Testament. It is important to understand that the complete subject matter of this particular chapter is idolatry or the worship of idols. The entire **Chapter 10** is an exhortation by God of advice about that which is good and right by contrasting examples against idolaters who have created traditions and objects of worship instead of worshiping our heavenly Father.

We can never take Him out of the equation. An idol of worship could be a boat, car, house, hunting property, the pursuit of wealth, a business, a Christmas tree, or even Satan himself if we allow it.

STUDY 6

Naturally we should never allow anything to come between ourselves and our love for God. We are to love our heavenly Father with all our heart, soul, and mind. This is the greatest commandment **(Matthew 22:37–38)**.

We do not worship the Christmas tree, but we can appreciate its beauty and sense of nature as an evergreen or everlasting tree year around in contrast to other trees, which lose their leaves during the winter months. In fact, our heavenly Father uses this very same symbolism in describing Himself spiritually as "a green fir tree" **(Hosea 14:9)**. In His comparison, He reminds us of His fruitfulness provided, as well as His protection, and His grace (love) forever. He is my Tree, is He yours?

Levitical Food Laws

From the very beginning of God's creation of this earth age, some twelve thousand to fourteen thousand years ago, our heavenly Father has ensured our wellbeing, providing all the components necessary to maintain these flesh bodies over scores of generations past and present. Flesh is the same today as it was yesterday. Likewise, the flesh body's requirements for healthful nutrition have never changed.

God has provided us with oxygen, water, dry land, sunlight, grass, the self-sustaining herb yielding seed and trees yielding seeding fruit knowing these things were good. He gave us the stars and planets to create for us time—days, months, years, signs, and seasons. He gave us the light of the day in which to live our lives and the comfort of darkness to rest our bodies. He has provided us with cattle, fish of the waters, and fowl of the air for meat to eat. Our heavenly Father also created all manner of other living creatures—creeping, swarming, crawling, and animals of all types. Just as He provides for us, so does He also provide for all of the animals of the earth with green plants and meat to eat. Over all the earth and of these creatures, He gave us dominion. God's love for us has created our very existence and has ensured our wellbeing, security, and contentment. He reflected on all things He created and said, "Behold, it was very good" **(Genesis chapter 1)**. He created all things for His pleasure **(Revelation 4:11)**.

In accordance with God's will to replenish the earth **(Genesis 1:28)**, man's longevity had at one time measured in the hundreds of years **(Genesis chapter 5)**. Our Father ultimately placed a limit on the prolonged existence of flesh man at a hundred twenty years **(Genesis 6:3)**. During the next four thousand five hundred years, we see man's average life span decline until about the time of Moses

(1490 BC), leveling out between seventy and eighty years (**Psalms 90:10**) just as it is today.

God's love for us guaranteed nothing has been left to chance. Our Father gave us written instructions (the Bible), detailing how to live our lives to the fullest including the very foods created for us to eat to help keep us as healthy as possible. These written instructions related to healthy eating are found in the books of **Leviticus chapter 11** and **Deuteronomy 14:1–20**. Collectively, they are commonly referred to as "the Levitical Food Laws."

God's instructions of the "ordinances" required of the Levitical priesthood for the oblation of sin are written in the same book of **Leviticus.** The food laws submerged within are often considered part of the ceremony of sacrificial rituals conducted by the Levite priests. Consequently, some Christians think that they were annulled in as much as these sacrificial blood ordinances were made void upon the crucifixion of Jesus Christ (**Colossians 2:11–14**). The first five books written in the Old Testament are known as the "Book of Moses," "Pentateuch," or "Mosaic Laws." As such, today, they are ascribed generally to the Jewish religion as a whole including the food laws within. Christians often fail to give them their deserved and complete justification much beyond their historical importance. The fact is the Pentateuch is referred to at least 1531 times throughout all the books of the prophets (Old Testament). Jesus and His disciples (New Testament) refer countless times to the Pentateuch. Jesus tells us:

> **Think not that I am come to destroy the law, or the prophets; I am not come to destroy, but to fulfil. For verily I say unto you, till heaven and earth pass, one jot or one tittle shall in no wise pass from the law, till all be fulfilled. (Matthew 5:17–18)**

Biblical laws consist of four general categories—commandments, statutes, judgements, and ordinances. The word *"law"* is derived from old Hebrew in origin and means to point the way or point out. *"Ordinances"* are ceremonial rituals. A *"commandment"* is an order instructing moral conduct. *"Statutes"* are an established rule or law defined in writing. *"Judgements"* are decisions rendered through discernment of governing laws.

The Levitical food laws have nothing to do with the ceremonial rituals of the sacrificial ordinances just as God's Ten Commandments have nothing to do with these ceremonial ordinances. Yet as God's laws, the food laws are not arbitrary, subject to one's opinion, judgement, or prejudices. The food laws are not ordered commandments of God which, when violated, result in civil or spiritual condemnation having sinned against God. However, violation of the food laws does result in sinning against our own bodies subjecting ourselves to unnecessary adverse influences.

God's simplicity is straightforward:

> **This is the law of the beasts, and of the fowl, and of every living creature that moveth in the waters, and every creature that creepeth upon the earth. To make a difference between the unclean and the clean and between the beast that may be eaten and the beast that may not be eaten. (Leviticus 11:46–47)**

> **What? Know ye not that your body is the temple of the Holy Spirit which is in you, which ye have of God, and ye are not your own? For ye are bought with a price; therefore glorify God in your body, and in your Spirit, which are Gods. (1 Corinthians 6:19–20)**

The Levitical food laws are provided for all believers as is the entire Bible by our heavenly Father to point the way for us, His children, through His wisdoms. In this instance, He teaches us how to properly nourish and maintain our bodies in a healthy manner to help reduce the risk of disease, illness, and disability. The result is a longer, happier life in service to God.

STUDY 7

Only within the most recent hundred years or so have our dietary sciences brought forth the importance of the foods we eat and the significant role they play in determining our overall health and wellbeing including the recently discovered dangers associated with certain pesticides and genetically modified (GMO) seed and food.

From the very beginning of creation, God taught us that plants which are to be eaten as a food source consist of herbs of the type which yield seeds **(Genesis 1:11–12, 29)**. The list of these plant types is extensive and may vary greatly depending on the region of their origin. Some of the more familiar ones within the United States are peas, sweetcorn, beans, collard, pumpkin, cucumber, lettuce, squash, peppers, radishes, tomatoes, potatoes, broccoli, cauliflower, celery, spinach, kohlrabi, cabbage, turnip, okra, etc.

A few popular items eaten today which are examples of a non-seed-bearing type plant are kelp, an algae propagated by root or tuber system, and mushrooms, a fungi propagated by spores. The list of non-seed-bearing plants continues on with seaweed, ferns, mosses, liverworts, to name a few. At this point, give some thought as to the environment some of these seedless plants most often grow and the bacteria often associated with their source. Let common sense dictate their total worth to the human body and, if any, whether or not that value can't be provided from another source. It is a well-known fact that some of these will even kill us. Our heavenly Father certainly created them all for a purpose—insects, reptiles, etc.—but not all as food for man.

Fruits created by our heavenly Father as a food source to be consumed by man consist of fruit trees yielding fruit after its kind whose seed is in itself **(Genesis 1:11–12, 29)**. Here too, there are many examples throughout the world, but some of the most common are apple, banana, pineapple, orange, pear, olive, pecan, grapefruit, cherry, peach, grape, mango, cashew, plum, avocado, pomegranate, coconut, papaya, almond, lychee, fig, lemon, gooseberry, key lime, etc.

During the time of Moses, the Hebrews divided earth's animal kingdom into four general groups: (1) land animals, (2) water animals, (3) birds of the air, and (4) swarming animals.

The Hebrew word *beast* has two meanings governed by how the word is used. The word *beast* (#929) can mean a four-legged animal such as cattle. However, the word *beast* (#2416) can also pertain to living creatures or animals of all types.

Beginning with category one above, "beasts of the earth" or land animals, the meat source God has approved for human consumption is at once restricted to "whatsoever parteth the hoof, and is cloven-footed, **and** cheweth the cud, among the beasts, that shall ye eat" **(Leviticus 11:3)**.

An animal with a cloven hoof, parted hoof, or cloven-footed is one with a split or cleft hoof (foot) such as cattle. Cleft is a past tense and past participle of the word *cleve*, meaning divided partially or completely by a fissure (a crevice or narrow opening) defining two halves.

An animal that "cheweth the cud" is one that is able to force up its food into the mouth from the first stomach (rumen) of a ruminant which is an animal with four stomach cavities capable of chewing their food over again as do cattle including other wild Bovidae such as the aurochs or urus of northern Africa and parts of Europe. The following are examples of other cloven hoof and cud chewing animals approved by our Father as a source of meat for our consumption located in **Deuteronomy 14:4–5**—ox, sheep, goat, hart (red deer), roebuck (gazelle), fallow deer (small European deer), wild goat, pygarg (mountain goat), wild ox (antelope), chamois (mountain sheep).

Samples of animals which have one or the other qualifications but not both begins in **Leviticus 11:4–8** and **Deuteronomy 14:7–8** are camel, coney (rock badger), hare, which chew the cud but do not have divided hoofs, and swine, which have the divided hoof but do not chew a cud.

"And whatsoever goeth upon his paws, among all manner of beasts that go on all four, these are unclean unto you" **(Leviticus 11:27)** which include dog, cat, lion, leopard, bear, wolf, coyote, hyena, etc.

STUDY 7

Next, from category two above is "water animals." This classification is greatly simplified by our Father in **Leviticus 11:9–12**:

> **[T]hese shall you eat of all that are in the waters; whatsoever hath fins and scales in the waters, in the seas, and in the rivers, them shall ye eat. And all that have not fins and scales in the seas, and in the rivers, of all that move in the waters, and of any living thing which is in the waters; they shall be an abomination unto you. They shall be even an abomination unto you; ye shall not eat of their flesh, but ye shall have their carcasses in abomination. Whatsoever hath no fins nor scales in the waters that shall be an abomination unto you.**

The Hebrew word *abomination* (#8262, #8263, #8241) means to be filthy, loathe, pollute, detest utterly, an idolatrous object, or something disgusting depending on its use.

There are many examples of "animals of the water" which do not have fins or scales as some fish do. Some of the more popular ones today are shrimp, lobster, oyster, clam, shark, octopus, snails, eel, crawfish, crabs, catfish, etc.

In category three "birds of the air," we read from **Deuteronomy 14:11**, "of all clean birds ye shall eat." The clarification of this simple statement is provided by the vast list specifying the unclean birds of the air which are not to be eaten as established in both **Leviticus 11:13–19** and **Deuteronomy 14:12–20**. The word *fowl* is introduced in these scriptures which is defined as (#5775) birds with feathers covered with wings. The list of unclean birds consist of eagle, ossifrage (#5822, sea eagle), osprey, glede (#7201, vulture), kite, vultures after their kind (family), raven after its kind (family), owl (little and great), nighthawk and hawk after their kind (family), cuckow (#7828, gull), swan, pelican, cormorant, stork, heron after their kind (family), lapwing (#1744, hoopoe), and the bat. Of birds considered clean to eat (not listed above) are pheasant, chicken, turkey, etc.

Category four brings us to the "swarming animals" of **Leviticus 11:20–23**—"all fowls that creep" (#8318) meaning a swarm or an active mass of minute animals. Creeping creatures "going upon all four, shall be an abomination unto you," we don't eat them. This group generally references the insect world of things that fly similar to mosquito, bee, knat, dragonfly, common housefly, June bug, and thousands of others. However there is an exception to these "flying creeping thing that goeth upon all four," which are those that "have legs above their feet, to leap withal upon the earth" **(v. 21)**. Of these creatures, those that we may eat are "locust after his kind [swarming], and the bald locust after his kind [devouring], and the beetle after his kind [chargol or wingless locust], and the grasshopper after his kind. But all other flying creeping things which have four feet shall be an abomination unto you" **(vv. 22–23)**.

Additional examples of "creeping" things which we are not to eat include weasel, mouse, and the tortoise after his kind, the ferret, chameleon, lizard, snail, and mole **(Leviticus 11:29–30)**. "Whatsoever goeth upon the belly, and whatsoever goeth upon all four, or whatsoever hath more feet among all creeping things that creep upon the earth, them ye shall not eat; for they are an abomination" **(Leviticus 11:42)**—snake, spider, worm, grub, etc.

Our Father also incorporates written instructions concerning the importance of food sanitation and hygiene in keeping a clean work environment through the washing of hands, utensils, clothing, and surfaces used in the handling and preparation of meat **(Leviticus 11:24–40; Deuteronomy 14:7–8)**. He also instructs us not to eat fat nor blood **(Leviticus 3:17)**.

As a quick "rule-of-thumb" as to which animals are not meant to be eaten by mankind, whether land, water, bird, or swarming, if considered a scavenger, don't eat them.

As an illustration, swine (pig) is a land animal God purposed as a scavenger to help keep the earth clean from wastes. We know today that swine do not have sweat glands (except a few within their snouts) thus are unable to completely rid their bodies of ingested toxins with these toxins ending up stored in their flesh. Pawed animals (dog, cat, coyote, wolf, hyena, etc.) scavenge the earth for rodents, carcasses,

STUDY 7

and other rubbishes. Aquatic animals other than finned and scaled fish vacuum the seas, lakes, and rivers, sifting them of decay, toxins, pollutants, and other contaminants detrimental to our health.

Another memory tool one may find useful is within the letters *P, N, B,* and *C. P* for priority—learn to give priority to good wholesome foods in your diet. *N* for natural—think along the lines of the natural foods avoiding processed foods when possible. *B* is for balance, bringing together a healthy combination of all the food groups. *C* is common sense, remembering we are what we eat.

Consider these two Bible verses with what we have now learned:

1. In the book of **Isaiah** (Old Testament), God is angered by man's continued disobedience against him. Included in His list of grievances is man's violation of His food law which states in part: "[W]hich remain among the graves, and lodge in the monuments, which eat swine's flesh, and broth of abominable things is in their vessels" **(Isaiah 65:45)**.
2. The Apostle Paul writes a warning: "[T]hat in latter times some shall depart from the faith giving heed," including "abstain from meats which God hath created to be received" **(1 Timothy 4:1–3)**. The word *received* (Greek #3335/3336) as used here means "accepted, used, to eat."

God's Elect

Different names are used throughout the Bible identifying God's elect, such as; saints, anointed, chosen, first fruits, and remnant, to name a few, but all are referencing a selection of His children for His purpose.

God's elect are brought forth in many places throughout the Bible to make complete God's will.

> **And I will bring forth a seed out of Jacob, and out of Judah an inheritor of My mountains; and Mine elect shall inherit it, and My servants shall dwell there. (Isaiah 65:9)**

> **And we know that all things work together for good to them that love God, to them who are the called, according to His purpose. (Romans 8:29)**

From the very beginning and all through history, God has chosen men and women to perform tasks in order to fulfill His purpose—Adam and Eve, the bloodline from which Jesus would come, Noah and his family to preserve the bloodline from an evil world, the prophets and prophetess to guide and direct His people, Moses to lead His people, apostles and preachers to teach His Word throughout the four corners of the earth and to preach the good news of salvation. Even today, from positions of great to small, we see God's love and grace daily, through those that serve Him.

STUDY 8

God's elect were chosen by Him before this earth age. Speaking to Jeremiah, God says:

> **Before I formed thee in the belly I knew thee; and before thou camest forth out of the womb I sanctified thee, and I ordained thee a prophet unto the nations. (Jeremiah 1:5)**

Paul, an apostle of Jesus Christ, speaking to the "saints":

> **According as He hath chosen us in Him before the foundation of the world, that we should be holy and without blame before Him in love. Having predestinated us unto the adoption of children by Jesus Christ to Himself. (Ephesians 1:4–5)**

Peter includes in his address of greetings, the elect:

> **Elect, according to the foreknowledge of God the Father, through sanctification of the Spirit, unto obedience and sprinkling of the blood of Jesus Christ. (1 Peter 1:2)**

And unto the Christians of the world:

> **For whom He did foreknow, He also did predestinate to be conformed to the image of His Son, that He might be the first born among many brethren. Moreover whom He did predestinate, them He also called; and whom He called, them He also justified; and whom He justified, them He also glorified. (Romans 8:29–30)**

God allows freewill to everyone so that each must choose good or evil—to love our Father or Satan. However, God will intercede with the freewill of His elect.

> **"And He that searcheth the hearts knoweth what is the mind of the Spirit because He maketh intercession for the saints according to the will of God" (Romans 8:27).**

A couple of examples of God's intercessions with His elect will include Jonah and the great fish. God wanted Jonah to go to Nineveh to preach and Jonah refused. The ship's crew threw him overboard during a great storm where he was swallowed by a fish for three days and spewed out on the shore where he did preach, and a great many repented of their evil ways **(Jonah chapter 1)**.

Another great example is Paul himself, once Saul, whose mission was, by order of the high priest, to destroy the disciples of the Lord (church), imprison and kill Jews, men or women, when God struck him down on the road to Damascus. Paul, a chosen vessel unto God **(Acts 9:15)**, became one of Jesus's disciples and an apostle unto the Gentiles, kings, and children of Israel.

Even today, in our personal lives, have you ever wondered why you moved to a place you never thought you would live or seemed to be led to change churches or jobs? Have you ever been moved to witness to someone out of the blue? If we think back for a moment, it becomes obvious to each of us how God has interceded in our lives for His will, even on the smallest of scales, for the larger picture. Have you ever been thrown in harm's way only to miraculously escape unscathed? Have you ever been studying God's Word and suddenly the "light bulb went on" where your eyes and ears were opened to understanding?

> **For the children being not yet born, neither having done any good or evil, that the purpose of God according to election might stand, not of works, but of Him that calleth. (Romans 9:11)**

STUDY 8

As believers in Jesus Christ, Christians, God's elect have a special destiny in these end times too.

> **And it shall come to pass in the last days, saith God, I will pour out of My Spirit upon all flesh; and your sons and your daughters shall prophesy, and your young men shall see visions, and your old men shall dream dreams. (Acts 2:17)**

As God's elect, our job during Satan's tribulation period is to stand before Satan and give testimony against him. We must be prepared.

> **Wherefore take unto you the whole armor of God, that ye may be able to withstand in the evil day** [the hour of temptation, detailed in **Revelation chapter 17**], **and having done all, to stand. (Ephesians 6: 13)**

Jesus explains to His disciples the order of things to come in the end times including:

> **But take heed to yourselves for they shall deliver you up to councils; and in the synagogues ye shall be beaten; and ye shall be brought before rulers and kings for My sake for a testimony against them. And the gospel must first be published among all nations. But when they shall lead you and deliver you up, take no thought beforehand what ye shall speak, neither do ye premeditate; but whatsoever shall be given you in that hour** [the hour of temptation] **that speak ye; for it is not ye that speak, but the Holy Spirit. (Mark 13:9–11)**

This is the unforgiveable sin spoken of in **Luke 12:10–12**. Again in **Revelation**, God tells us (the church) that we are not to be afraid, that He knows of those who say they are Jews (Christians) but are not. Rather they are from the synagogue of Satan.

> **Fear none of those things which thou shalt suffer; behold, the devil shall cast some of you into prison, that ye may be tried; and ye shall have tribulation ten days; be thou faithful unto death, and I will give thee a crown of life. (Revelation 2:10)**

God knows He can count on His elect, His Christian soldiers, to stand before Satan during his "hour" to give testimony against him (Satan) through the Holy Spirit. We have earned this honor and privilege to serve our Father in any role He has chosen for us during these end times in order that His will be accomplished. As God's elect, we have a special destiny in these times, and we need to be ready spiritually.

An overview of the sequence of events of the end times is laid before us by Jesus in **Mark chapter 13 (also Mathew chapter 24 and Luke chapter 21).** Jesus warns "Now learn the parable of the fig tree" **(Mark 13:28)** which is written in **Jeremiah chapter 24**. It is the prophecy of Israel being reborn once again as a nation which historically occurred in 1948. God's people are returning to their promised land, a new nation as prophesied again in **Ezekiel 37: 18–25**. This event marks the beginning of the last generation entering the end-times. The book of **Revelation** reveals the end times in detail.

Parable of the Fig Tree

Jesus frequently spoke in parables, which are narratives of abstract ideas with human attributes inherent to a person or thing. Jesus often spoke utilizing analogies associated with farming practices and nature. Parables express a resemblance in essentials between two things or statements otherwise different. One of the reasons Jesus exercised this method of instruction is in His knowledge that the concepts of these basics would transcend generations of time and languages all over the world.

The Greek word *parabole* (3850) means a fictitious narrative of common life conveying a moral adage or comparison. In the Hebrew language, the word is *mashal* (4912), meaning a sense of superiority in mental action, usually a metaphor (figure of speech) of nature, an adage, or poem. In English, the word means a short narrative making a moral or religious point by comparison with a natural or homely thing.

When Jesus's disciples questioned Him as to why He spoke in parables, Jesus responded with the most important reason in a very detailed teaching moment **(Matthew 13:10–23)**. Simply paraphrased, to the disciples and those that love the Lord, it is given to know the mysteries of the kingdom of heaven, but to others, it is not. The use of parables also fulfilled the prophecy of **Isaiah 6:9–10**: "[P]eople will hear but not understand and see but are unable to perceive." People's hearts and minds are closed to our loving Father and His Word, the Bible. However, to those who seek Him will they begin to understand God's mystery of His kingdom (salvation), and God will convert and heal them. Jesus continues to detail this subject to his disciples (and us) with the parable of the sower **(Matthew**

13:18–23), adding that those who gain in understanding continue on in telling others of the "good news" of Jesus Christ.

Jesus resumes educating His disciples with the parable of the "tares" (2215, Greek meaning "darnel or false grain") which relate to these things that have been kept secret since the beginning of the world **(Matthew 13:24–35)**. However, still unsure of the implication, the disciples again ask Jesus to explain its meaning in further detail, which Jesus does, as presented in **Matthew 13:36–52**. It is just as important for us at this time to take a moment to read these passages that we might gain understanding as they relate to comprehending the end of this world age and provide the background to our study of the "Parable of the Fig Tree."

The interrelationship of the four Gospels **(Matthew, Mark, Luke, and John)** is in the presentation of Jesus—as King, as servant, as man, and as God respectively. The divine purpose is to give us four aspects of Jesus's life on earth and His death. Therefore, you will see that the books of **Matthew chapter 24, Mark chapter 13,** and **Luke chapter 21** are parallel writings pertaining to our subject matter but vary slightly regarding their aspects of presentation. To obtain a well-rounded perspective in recognizing the signs of the end of this earth age, we need to read all three postures.

The focus here in our study is that in each of these three narratives where Jesus is explaining the warning signs of the end times, He very clearly and emphatically in all three accounts tells us to *"learn a parable of the fig tree"* **(Matthew 24:32; Mark 13:28; Luke 21:29)**. Jesus doesn't "suggest" or "recommend" that we may not "want" or "wish" to learn of the parable nor does He state it once or twice, but three times, each in witness to the other! Why? To ensure that we realize the importance of knowing when the end times unmistakably begin ("know that summer is near") and that "this generation **shall not pass** til **all** these things be done" **(Matthew 24:34; Mark 13:30; Luke 21:32)**.

In the Old Testament, God becomes very angry with His chosen people, Israel, because they continually disobey Him. After many warnings **(Deuteronomy chapters 28 to 30,** circa 1490 BC), God eventually divides the house of Israel and scatters the two tribes of

STUDY 9

Judah and the ten tribes of Israel throughout the world **(Zechariah 7:12–14)**. World history records this event beginning in about 600 BC. God also stated that He will one day in the future gather His people, reuniting Judah and Israel, back together again **(Ezekiel 37:19–28)**.

We find the parable of the fig tree written in **Jeremiah 24:1–7**. God explains the parable of the fig tree to his prophet Jeremiah. It is the regathering of God's chosen people, both good and bad figs from around the world. and returning them back to their promised land of Israel.

This promised prophecy came to pass following World War II. On May 8, 1948, the world community, through the United Nations, authorized and recognized the re-establishment of the nation of Israel.

During the past seventy years since Israel's rebirth, we have been witnesses to the fulfillment of God's prophecy in the gathering of the Jewish people and their return to Israel. The rebuilding of Israel as a nation has been on going ever since, exactly as foretold by God. Historically speaking, previous to 1948, the name "Israel" hadn't appeared on any map nor had it existed as a country for nearly two thousand five hundred years!

> **Now learn a parable of the fig tree; when her branch is yet tender and putteth forth leaves, ye know that summer is near.**
>
> **So ye in like manner, when ye shall see these things come to pass, know that it is nigh, even at the doors.**
>
> **Verily, I say unto you that this generation shall not pass til all these things be done. (Mark 13:28–30)**

Keep in mind that the subject in each of these parts of the three books **(Mathew chapter 24, Mark chapter 13, and Luke chapter 21)** is Jesus's summary of the signs which usher in the end of this world age **(Matthew 24:3)**. Briefly, they are the destruction of the temple, great lies deceiving many, wars, rumors of war, famines, pestilences, earthquakes in different places, Christians will be hated, people will betray and hate one another, false teachers will increase in numbers and will deceive many, lawlessness will abound, and the hearts of man will become indifferent, but those strong in Christ will be saved. The gospel will be preached to all the world, and then the end begins. Satan is thrown from heaven onto the earth (at the sixth trump) as the antichrist ("anti" in Greek meaning "instead of"), entering peacefully and prosperously **(Daniel 8:23–25)**. He is capable of performing miraculous signs as a supernatural being **(Revelation 13:13–15)**, deceiving many. Fortunately for mankind, Satan's reign of tribulation is shortened to a five-month period **(Revelation 9:5)**. Then, following the seventh trump, the second advent of Christ's triumphant return takes place **(Mark 13:26)**, wiping out evil once and for all eternity. For those of us here throughout these tribulation periods, it is reassuring to know that as believers and followers of Christ (Christians), we have nothing to fear as our heavenly Father watches over His own **(Luke 21:36)**.

A deeper study of the end times is necessary for a thorough understanding of these things which is not the intent of this study. Here, only the "season" of the signs is intended to be brought forth. With the knowledge of the "Parable of the Fig Tree," God has provided us with the season knowing that "this generation shall not pass until all is fulfilled."

The Bible defines "generation" with three different periods of time—a hundred twenty years **(Genesis 6:3)**, seventy years **(Psalms 90:10)**, and forty years **(Numbers 14:28–35)**. Since the year 1948, we can see those forty years have already passed and that we have now entered into the seventy-year definition. We need only look to the Middle East today, the behavior of peoples of the world in which we live, world political troubles, and economic failures to see that the stage is being set.

Jesus says that no man, angel, nor even He knows the hour of His return—only God Himself **(Mark 13:32)**. Therefore watch **(Matthew 24:42)**, be ready **(Matthew 24:44)**, take heed, watch, and

STUDY 9

pray **(Mark 13:33)**. What Jesus has told His disciples, He is telling everyone **(Mark 13:37)**.

Don't be deceived—take notice of God's warning signs that He has provided to us in His Word. Consider the clear evidence all around us today. Watch, pray, and be ready.

"For God so loved the world, that He gave His only Begotten Son, that whosoever believeth in Him should not perish, but have everlasting life" **(John 3:16)**.

ANGELS
PART 1 (SPIRITUAL BEINGS)

Introduction

Since the beginning of this earth age, we (mankind) have struggled to understand a supernatural world, supernatural beings, and their existence in a supernatural dimension invisible from our natural world.

Between the speculative sciences, metaphysical theories, reports of extraterrestrial activities, and the never-ending technological discoveries of today, the idea of the supernatural is now more seriously regarded by most in the scientific world, if not accepted as fact.

The word *supernatural* means something occurring or existing outside of the normal experience or knowledge of man, caused by other than the known forces of nature, beyond natural forces, the miraculous, or divine.

This search of the Bible is to uncover the truths of that which God's Word has been teaching us for thousands of years about the living beings of another dimension, invisible from our own **(Colossians 1:15–17)**, known to us as "angels." However, this study does not include the "fallen angels," "familiar spirits" (evil spirits), or angels of evil morals due to the immensity of the subject and is reserved for an independent study at another time.

To help with the accuracy of our study, it is imperative that we go back to the original languages in which the Bible is written—Hebrew, Greek, and Aramaic. Etymology, the study of the origin of words and the way their meaning have changed throughout history, isn't anything new. Noah Webster was keenly aware of the dangers of misinterpretations and serious errors possible when original meanings are ignored. About 240 years ago, he stated (in part):

> **In the lapse of two or three centuries, changes have taken place which obscures the sense of the original languages. The effect of these changes is that some words are now used in a sense different from that which they had and thus present a wrong signification or false idea. (Noah Webster, the Holy Bible with amendments of the language [New Haven: Durrie and Peck, 1833, p.iii])**

Another fact of truth that we must be cognitive of is many times, humans and our finite languages are often unable to find words to express infinite realities.

Therefore, in this report, the definition of Hebrew words of the Old Testament or Greek words of the New Testament will be followed by numbers(s) in parentheses as assigned by *The Strong's Exhaustive Concordance of the Bible* (Authorized King James Version) for the purpose of ready references.

Definitions

The word *angel* in the Hebrew language is "malak" (4397), meaning to dispatch as a deputy, messenger, an angel, ambassador. The word *angel* in the Greek language is "aggelos/aggello" (32), meaning a messenger, an angel, to lead, bring forth, carry, and keep. In the English language, when used as a noun, the word *angel* literally means a messenger, a spirit, or spiritual being employed by God to communicate His will to man.

This word *spirit* in the English language is defined as a breath of air, air, wind, soul, supernatural being, as an angel (good or evil). In the Hebrew language, the word *spirit* is "ruwach" (7307), translated as mind, spirit, wind, breath or air. It may also be translated as "owb" (178, familiar [evil] spirit) or "neshamah" (5397, puff, wind, angry or vital breath, divine inspiration, intellect, soul, spirit). In the Greek language, the word *spirit* is "pneuma" (4151), translated as current of air, blow, breeze, superhuman, angel (good or evil), divine God, Holy Spirit, Christ's Spirit. It may also be "psuche" (5594), meaning rational and immortal soul (not likely to die), corresponding with the Hebrew word (7307) and (5315) mentioned earlier but also includes the Hebrew word *chay* (2416), meaning life, living creature, or thing.

From these definitions of "angel" and "spirit" above, used interchangeably in the Bible, we can determine collectively that an angel is a supernatural, spiritual being, of either good or evil moral, with an intelligent soul. They are a living immortal being (not likely to die), superhuman, of a supernatural spiritual body likened to the wind or air as invisible, a divine creature created by God to serve Him at this time as messengers between He and man in accordance with His will.

The word *angel(s)* is found 298 times in the Bible—117 times in the Old Testament and 181 times in the New Testament. In addition to these numbers, we must also be aware that uncounted biblical metaphors are also commonly used in the Bible to describe angelic beings such as "sons of God" **(Genesis 6:2)**, "sons of man" **(Daniel 10:16)**, "princes" **(Daniel 10:13)**, "beasts" **(Revelation 4:6)**, "saints" **(Zechariah 14:5)**, "holy ones" **(Daniel 4:13)**, "watchers" **(Daniel 4:13)**, "stars of heaven" **(Revelation 12:4)**, or "hosts" **(Jeremiah 33:22)**. A metaphor is a figure of speech or symbol in which a word or phrase which is applied to an object or action to which it is not literally applicable.

Viewpoint

Since medieval times, some have suggested that as many as nine different orders of celestial beings exist. This proposed order not only consists of the archangels, cherubim, seraphim, and angels as investigated herein but also includes dominions, powers, thrones, principalities, and authorities. A study of the definitions of the later five—dominions (Hebrew 4910, 4475, Greek 2961, 2904), powers (Greek 1411, 1849), thrones (Hebrew 3678, Greek 2362), principalities (Hebrew 4761, Greek 746), and authorities (Hebrew 7235, Greek 1849)—reveal all of these later five correlate with governmental communities, both on earth and in heaven of which Jesus Christ rules over all **(Ephesians 1:21–23; Colossians 1:16; 1 Peter 3:22; Romans 8:37–39)**. None of the above definitions relate to a particular type of supernatural being as do the first four—archangels, cherubim, seraphim, and angels. Therefore, this study will focus on these four groups specifically described as supernatural beings in God's Word, which of course, Jesus rules over as well.

Following the King of kings, Lord of lords, Jesus Christ **(Revelation 17:14)**, there appears to be a royal order established by God of spiritual beings within His invisible, supernatural world (heaven) just as He has established an order of flesh beings within His natural world (earth) where mankind has been given dominion **(Genesis 1:28)**.

The first echelon of known supernatural beings (angels) created by our heavenly Father seems to be the "archangels," followed by the "cherubim," then the "seraphim," all of which are supported by the massive number of the mainstream company of "angels." Each group of these spirit beings seems to have a specific area of designated purpose or responsibility as commanded by God in addition to their overall collective charge as messengers between He and mankind.

Archangels

The term *archangel*, written only twice in the Bible, comes from the Greek word *archaggelos* (743), created from "arch" (757) and "aggelos" (32). Together, the word means chief angel, to be first in rank, reign over, and messenger angel.

Bible students may debate as to the actual number of archangels in existence, but the number seems to rest between four **(Revelation 7:1)** and seven **(Revelation 4:1)**. This will remain a deeper study for another time. Our study focuses on the two archangels shown to us in scripture named Michael and Gabriel.

Michael is clearly identified in the book of **Jude, verse 9** as an archangel. He is mentioned in the book of **Daniel 10:13, 21** while on earth as one of the chief princes (archangels) and shown standing up (defending) Daniel's people in this prophecy of end times. Later, Michael is seen at war in heaven against Satan and his angels prior to the second advent of Jesus Christ, in which Michael and his angels prevail, casting Satan and his angels from heaven to the earth **(Revelation 12:7–9)**. Michael is a messenger from God, of prophesy, a defender of the righteous, a warrior dispensing God's judgement, and leader of other angels.

The second archangel described in God's Word is Gabriel. Although not specifically titled "archangel" in scripture as Michael, Gabriel's identity as an archangel lies in his name itself. The Hebrew word for the proper noun "Gabriel" is *Gabriy-el* (1403). It is derived from the Hebrew words *gabar* (1396), *geber* (1397) and *El* (410). Collectively, his name means man of God, archangel, strong, great, mighty, valiant man, warrior, goodly, of a deity.

Gabriel is the first of the archangels to be formerly introduced in scripture **(Daniel 8:16)**. He is dispatched (circa 495 BC) by our heavenly Father to earth for the purpose of teaching Daniel skills in understanding his vision of the end-times prophecy **(Daniel 8:17)**. Approximately five hundred years later, Gabriel is dispatched by God to earth again to deliver God's message of good news to Zacharias, husband to Elisabeth, mother of John the Baptist **(Luke 1:7–19)**. Six months following, God again dispatches Gabriel to earth with a message of good news to Mary and the world, announcing her conception by the Holy Spirit and the birth of Jesus Christ, Son of God, into the world **(Luke 1:26–31)**.

Gabriel is a messenger of good news, wisdom, understanding, mercy, teaching, and promise. Through Gabriel, we learn that the archangels hold the prominent position of standing before the very throne of God **(Luke 1:19)**. We also see that their (the archangels') appearance is in the likeness of a man **(Ezekiel 1:5)**. Remember, God created us (man) in their (spiritual beings/angels) and His (God's) own likeness **(Genesis 1:26–27, 9: 6)**.

Cherub

The pronoun *cherub* or *cherubim* (plural) is mentioned ninety-one times in scripture. The Hebrew word is *kruwb* (3742); meaning Cherub or imaginary figure. The Greek word is *cheroubim* (5502), repeating the Hebrew word *cherub* or *cherubim* (3742). The

English translation for "cherubim" is just as nondescript, citing heavenly beings.

God's prophet Ezekiel (circa 484 to 465 BC) gives us a firsthand description of cherubim **(Ezekiel 10:1–20, 1:5–14)**. Jesus's disciple John provides an additional description approximately six hundred years later (96 AD) in the New Testament **(Revelation 4:6–9)**. Note here that John utilizes the metaphor "beast"—Greek word "zoa" (2198) or "zoon" (2226) meaning to live, a living thing, living ones, living creatures. With these descriptions and in **Genesis, 3:24**, we always see cherubim in close proximity beside our heavenly Father and His throne where, as celestial beings, appear to act as sentinels (keepers). The cherubim appear to take precedence first before the other angels and the twenty-four elders when approaching God's altar for prayer **(Revelation 6:9–14)**.

The cherubim, four in number **(Ezekiel 1:5)**, appear to serve as messengers dispensing God's wrath upon man and the earth, such as war, famine, death, and pestilence **(Revelation chapters 6 and 15:7)**. Satan himself was once a cherub, full of great wisdom and beauty serving God as a keeper over the mercy seat before sinning against God, resulting in his ultimate fall from God's grace **(Ezekiel chapter 28)**.

The appearance of a cherub is also in the likeness of a man **(Ezekiel 1:5)**. Let me remind you again that God created us (man) in their (spiritual beings) and His (God's) own likeness **(Genesis 1:26–27)**. With this knowledge in mind, we know that Satan does not have horns, tail, red suit, or wings, etc. God created Satan the most beautiful, highly intelligent, full of wisdom, with supernatural powers **(Ezekiel chapter 28)**.

Scripture does not support the popular misgiving that angels have "wings" allowing them to "fly." This image comes from the descriptions of an angelic beings' capability to move from one location to another instantly at high speeds, a supernatural capability. For thousands of years, mankind has had no other way to explain this supernatural phenomena until only recently, within the last hundred twenty years or so of man's eight-thousand-year existence on earth. We now understand man's capability to "fly" within objects designed with (or without) "wings" transporting us from one place to another at high speeds as birds of the sky "fly" with "wings." Again, our Father created us in their image. We do not have "wings" nor does our heavenly Father or the angels have "wings." Jesus walked on the earth in the flesh and, when asked, said, "[H]e that hath seen me, hath seen the Father" **(John 14:9)**.

Seraphim

The seraphim is the least revealed of the four groups of supernatural spirits in the Bible. They are only mentioned twice by name and with very few details **(Isaiah 6: 2, 6–7)**.

The name "seraphim" comes from the Hebrew word *saraph* (8414/8313) meaning on fire, burning, a symbolic creature of copper color, fiery (serpent).

We see the seraphim's ministry is giving praise to our Father, constantly glorifying Him **(Isaiah 6:3)** and purging sin from God's servants **(Isaiah 6:7)**. Their position in reference to God's throne is always above His throne while cherubim take their place beside His throne, and the archangels' position is standing before His throne.

The seraphim is the only supernatural being which is not specifically mentioned as "appearing in the likeness of man" as the archangels, cherubim, and other angels. Each of the two seraphim is described as having six wings, each with two wings covering his face, two wings covering his feet, and two wings used to fly, thereby maintaining their positions above God's throne.

Prior to the crucifixion of Jesus Christ, the keepers of God's throne ensured limited access to our Father. Since Jesus's resurrection, having defeated death, offering His own blood for the atonement (sacrifice) cleansing us of our sins, God rent (tore) the veil which had previously separated our uncleanliness from His holy throne so that now, through Jesus Christ, we have direct access to our Father day or night, twenty-four hours a day, seven days a week **(Matthew 27:50–51; Ephesians 2:18–19; Ephesians 3:11–12; Romans 5:2)**.

Between the three categories of angels we have investigated so far, we have only accounted for ten to thirteen supernatural beings

STUDY 10

of the "ten thousand times ten thousand" (a hundred million) and the "thousands times thousands" (Hebrew colloquialisms meaning countless numbers) which still exist **(Revelation 5:11 and Daniel 7:10)**. The "hosts of heaven" (stars of heaven—angels), cannot be numbered **(Jeremiah 33:22)**.

We know now that God created us in the image of His spiritual beings, including Himself **(Genesis 1:26–27)** and that we look like each other—human beings and spiritual beings **(Ezekiel 1:5; Genesis 19:1–5; Daniel 8:15, 10:18)**. God created all things in heaven and earth, visible and invisible **(Colossians 1:16)**, that which we can see (this dimension) and that which we cannot see (another dimension). God can make the invisible (spiritual angels) visible to animals **(Numbers 22:23)** and mankind alike **(Numbers 22:31; Matthew 28:2–5; Genesis 32:1–2; Daniel 10:5–7; Revelation 10:1)** and even an army of many angels **(2 Kings 6:17)**. As we can see, the Bible is simply filled with information concerning the natural and the supernatural worlds about us.

Angels

The majority of God's supernatural beings fall under this grouping—by the billions. What follows is a list of only some of the things we know about them.

Angels excel in strength as supernatural beings **(Psalms 103:20)**.

Angels may be assigned to keep guard or watch over believers against plagues, evil, and give us support lest we dash our foot against a stone or any other dangers in our paths **(Psalms chapter 91)**.

Angels are "watchers" (Chaldee word "iyr," 5894) watching over the affairs of men **(Daniel 4:17)**.

Angels are ministering (serving) spirits sent by God to those heir to salvation (believers) **(Hebrews 1:14)**.

Angels are more intelligent than man **(2 Samuel, 14: 20)**.

However, angels don't know everything **(Mark 13:32)**.

The Apostle Paul had the spiritual gift of "tongues," meaning he could speak several languages including Latin, Hebrew, Greek, and even the language of angels, suggesting angels speak a different language than man **(1 Corinthians 13:1)**.

Angels are capable of eating man's food, such as bread, butter, milk, and beef **(Genesis 18:1–8, 19:3)**.

Man is capable of eating angels' food (manna), used by our Father to sustain the Israelites during their exodus from Egypt **(Psalms 78:24–25)**.

There is joy in heaven by the angels over one sinner that repenteth **(Luke 15:10)**.

God's Holy Spirit convicts us of our sins, not angels **(John 16:8)**.

Man is not to worship angels. Angels are our fellow servants to Almighty God and our brothers in Jesus Christ **(Revelation 19:10, 22:8–9)**.

We will judge angels **(1 Corinthians 6:3)**.

On earth, man is a little lower than the angels but are made equal to them at our resurrection **(Luke 20:36)**.

Our Angelic Connection

Angels are God's "children" **(Luke 20:36)**. He (God) created the "sons of God" (angels) **(Job 1:6)**, His "morning stars," and all sang together in joy **(Job 38:7)**. Here, our Father is reminding Job of the first heaven and earth age before Satan's fall from His grace. *Note*: for an abbreviated explanation of the three earth and heaven ages, read **2 Peter chapter 3**. For a deeper understanding, refer to a previous Bible study entitled "The Three Heaven and Earth Ages."

We, as God's children, are partakers of flesh and blood, as did Jesus. God doesn't ask us to do anything He Himself wouldn't do **(Hebrews 2:14–15)**.

Jesus came down from heaven **(John 6:38)**, born from above through the womb in flesh body, and returned to heaven **(John 7:33–34)** in spiritual body—as will His followers (believers) **(John 6:38–40)**.

While on earth, Jesus was also subjected to becoming a little lower than the angels **(Hebrews 2:7, 9; Psalms 8:5)**.

Man cannot enter heaven unless he is first born from "above" through the womb as He was **(John 3:1–7)**. *Note*: the word *again* in the KJV is mistranslated from the Greek word *anothen* (509), which properly translated means "above."

No man goes to heaven that didn't come down from heaven just as Jesus did **(John 3:12–13)**.

We have two bodies—our flesh bodies and our spiritual bodies within us **(1 Corinthians 15:44)**.

Bodies of flesh and blood cannot enter the supernatural dimension of heaven **(1 Corinthians 15:50)**. The entire **fifteenth chapter of 1 Corinthians** should be read for a deeper understanding of this part of our supernatural transition.

Angels are spiritual beings **(Hebrews 1:7; Revelation 1:4)**.

When the flesh body dies, our spiritual body instantly returns to our Father in heaven who created it **(Ecclesiastes 12:6–7; 2 Corinthians 5:6–7)** where we await on one side of the gulf or the other of "Abraham's bosom" ("paradise") until judgement day **(Luke 16:19–31)**.

Jesus tells us that when our spiritual bodies rise from the dead, they neither marry nor are given in marriage but are as the angels which are in heaven; neither can they die anymore and are the children of God, being the children of the resurrection **(Luke 20:34–36; Mark 12:25)**.

Our Father is the God of the living, not the dead **(Mark 12:27)**.

> **But for as many as received Him, to them gave He power to become the sons [children] of God, even to them that believe on His name. (John 1:12)**

> **For God so loved the world, that He gave His only begotten Son that whosoever believeth in Him should not perish, but have everlasting life. (John 3:16)**

Angels
Part 2
(The Fallen Angels)

Introduction

The events studied here are not to be confused with Satan's initial rebellion of the first heaven and earth age known as the "katabolle," in which our heavenly Father cast Satan and his followers out of heaven **(Revelation 12:1–4)**. Refer to the earlier study of "The Three Earth and Heaven Ages" for more on that subject. This study of "The Fallen Angels" takes place during the beginning period of this second earth and heaven age we live in now.

This continued study of angels (part 2) looks at the exploits of Satan's soldiers known as "the fallen angels" and their wickedness inflicted on the human race during two of their previous invasions of earth as subsequent actions to their main objective of attempting to sabotage the genealogical seed-line of Jesus Christ **(Luke 3:23–38)**. We will also clearly understand God's purpose in warning us against their third and final influx (invasion) of the earth in the future. Being forewarned of an event offers us the opportunity to prepare ourselves by having faith in God through education **(Acts 26:24–29)**. His purpose of prophecy is also His means of presenting undeniable truths. All biblical prophecies to date have come to fulfillment just as commanded by our heavenly Father and chronicled in His Word and history that we might believe on Him. Prophecies are not of men but of the Holy Spirit of God **(1 Peter 1:20–21)**.

STUDY 11

The English term *fallen angels* comes from the Hebrew root word *naphal* (#5307) meaning to fall, throw down, fallen and the plural *nephilim* meaning fallen ones.

Shortly after God created Adam and Eve in the garden of Eden, Satan began his attempts to destroy flesh man. Satan continued his attempts on at least fifteen separate occasions during the next four-thousand-year period, not only to destroy the adamic seed-line through the human race but also the very life of Jesus Himself. In each of these instances, God's direct intervention was necessary to ensure His plan for the salvation of His children is preserved through His Savior Jesus Christ.

Although each of these events is recorded in God's Word, man has seemingly been oblivious to Satan's persistent and ultimate motive behind his struggles. Satan desires to be worshipped as God—to be God, by any means he believes possible **(Ezekiel 28:1–2)**. This ongoing tumultuous conflict between God and Satan (Lucifer, son of the morning) subduing and weakening the nations of the world initiated with Satan's desire to be the "Most High" **(Isaiah 14:12–14)**.

The First Influx

In direct disobedience to God, the most ardent and devoted followers of Satan had refused to remain in their own place of habitation, the dimension in which they lived **(Jude 1:6)**. They traveled to earth around 3194 BC, about the time Adam was eight hundred ten years old or perhaps even earlier. This is calculated from the year of Adam's creation (4,004 BC) and the fact that Enoch the Prophet was born when Adam was eight hundred ten years old, circa 3194 BC. Enoch was two hundred forty-six years old, and his ministry was already well established, preaching against the Nephilim and their evil **(Jude 1:14–16)** when Noah was born in 2948 BC. The flood of Noah took place in the year 2348 BC when Noah was six hundred years old **(Genesis 7:6)**. This would mean that the progeny of the Nephilim, the giants (Gibbors), had been well established on earth for at least eight hundred fifty years before Noah's flood and probably longer.

The earth was beginning to become populated by the time the Nephilim arrived **(Genesis 6:1)**; Enoch was already the seventh adamic generation from Adam **(Jude 1:14)**, not to mention the sixth day creation of mankind which began inhabiting the earth roughly two thousand years before Adam was created **(Genesis 1:26–28)**.

When the "Sons of God" (angels—the fallen ones) arrived on earth, they saw the daughters of man and how beautiful they were and took them at will, all that they wanted, as their wives **(Genesis 6:2)**. From the earlier study of "Angels Part 1," we learned that angels are supernatural spiritual beings of great strength and intelligence. They are superhuman, living creatures; who could stop them? In fact, it appears man joined with them as God conveyed in part: "[T]he wickedness of man was great in the earth, and that every imagination of the thoughts of his heart was only evil continually" **(Genesis 6:5)**.

From these unholy unions between the human female and the Nephilim arose a mutated offspring, which is neither fully human nor fully angelic called *Gibbors*, the Hebrew word (#1368) meaning powerful warrior, strong man, giant, of old, renown for ungodliness.

From this fact, we have to come to the realization that angels have mass. They are certainly created of a different material than flesh man, enabling them to cross between the dimensions and many other supernatural attributes, including an ability to procreate. We saw this in the garden of Eden when Satan, himself a cherub angelic being, beguiled (wholly seduced) Eve **(Genesis 3:13)**. We know Cain was of Satan's seed and not of Adam's seed from Cain's separate genealogy recorded in **Genesis 4:17–24**. Cain is not recorded in Adam's genealogy found in **Genesis 4:25–26 and Genesis chapter 5.** God makes this fact abundantly clear when we read:

> **There were giants in the earth in those days; and also after that, when the sons of God came in unto the daughters of men, and they bare children to them, the same became mighty men which were of old, men of renown. (Genesis 6:4)**

The word *giants* in Hebrew is "nephiyl" or "nephil" (#5303/5307), meaning tyrant, bully, or giant. We will also see the Hebrew words *Rapha* (#7497/7496), also meaning giant, deceased, dead, and *Raphaim* (#1051) meaning house of giant.

God was extremely wrought with grief in His heart by all this and the wickedness He witnessed on earth to the point that He was sorry He had made flesh man along with the beasts, creeping things, and fowls of the air **(Genesis 6:5–6)**.

However, God found grace in Noah, a family history unblemished by the wickedness and violence of the times brought about by the fallen angels. Noah's family was a pure pedigree, from the Hebrew word *tamiym* (# 8549/8552) meaning undefiled, perfect, clean. Noah's family was without blemish, the technical word for bodily and physical perfection. His family was the only uncorrupted flesh beings remaining who revered (loved) God **(Genesis 6:8–9)**. Therefore, God told Noah to build the ark for him and his family and two of every flesh, male and female, to be saved from the destruction of all other flesh on earth by flood waters **(Genesis 6:9–22)**. The year is now 2349 BC, Noah is 601 years old **(Genesis 8:13)**, and until then, the Gibbors (giants) had lived on earth for about 1,450 years.

The Second Influx

Reading again from the verse above regarding **Genesis 6:4**, we understand that there were giants on the earth in "*those days*," meaning the days prior to Noah's flood, giving credence to the fact that these giants had been around for a while. We also read from the above verse the words "*and also after that*," meaning after the flood of Noah's time, letting us know that there was a second influx of the Nephilim which continued producing these giants or Gibbors even after the flood.

Approximately 351 years after the flood, Abraham (Abram) was born (1996 BC) at Ur, a city in Chaldees (Iraq) **(Genesis 11:26–28)**. Abraham (Abram) continues the seed-line from which Jesus would come. God made a covenant with Abraham (Abram) that he would become the father of many nations **(Genesis 17:4)**. Abraham's

(Abram) great-grandsons would be the patriarchs of the twelve tribes of Israel **(Genesis chapters 29 and 30)**. When Abraham (Abram) was seventy-five years old (1921 BC), God told him to move his family to Canaan. Satan and the fallen angels, somehow having anticipating the eventual arrival of Abraham, had already been at work corrupting the population in the land of Canaan, which also included the kingdoms of Sodom and Gomorrah. Canaan consisted of ten different peoples or nations at the time, which included Gibbors living amongst the Perizzites, Rephaims, and the Canaanites **(Genesis chapter 15)**. The Gibbors were already established in this land, which would eventually become the promise land given to Moses and the Israelites by God in another four hundred thirty years, circa 1491 BC.

When Moses and the Israelites did enter this area as their promised land in 1451 BC, God gave strict instructions to annihilate these certain tribes (nations) who were the remnant of the Nephilim, described as "great and tall" and "which were also accounted giants" **(Deuteronomy 2:10–11)**. One such example is the kingdom of Bashan, ruled by King Og **(Deuteronomy 3:2)**. King Og's bed measured nine cubits long by four cubits wide—at least fifteen feet, nine inches long by seven feet wide **(Deuteronomy 3:11)**. (Note: a cubit is the measurement of a man's forearm from elbow to the tip of the middle finger which measures roughly between twenty-one to twenty-five inches.) In several cases, however, the Israelites failed to drive out all of these peoples as God had commanded such as the Canaanites **(Joshua 16:10)** and others **(Judges Chapter 1)**. Because of this, God told the Israelites that the remnant will "be as a thorn in your sides" **(Judges 2:3)**.

Many wars continued in this area during the next five hundred years, whittling away at the number of remaining giants and their ungodly, immoral ways that continued to corrupt the earth. David was born in 990 BC, later to be King David of Israel. At sixteen years of age, David killed Goliath, the giant of the Philistines **(1 Samuel 17:50)**. Goliath stood "six cubits and a span" **(1 Samuel 17:4)**. The "span" mentioned is one half of the length of a cubit, approximately ten and a half inches. From these measurements, we can determine that Goliath was somewhere between eleven feet, four inches to thirteen feet, six inches tall. King David battled against the last of the sons of giants when he was about sixty-seven years of age when he was almost killed, at which time his soldiers refused to let him go to war again **(2 Samuel 21:16–17)**. King David died approximately three years later about 920 BC. Beyond the recounting of these battles of King David in **1 Chronicles chapter 20,** the word *giant* is no longer mentioned in the Bible. "Yet destroyed I [God speaking] the Amorite before them, whose height was like the height of the cedars, and he was strong as the oaks; yet I destroyed his fruit from above, and his roots from beneath" **(Amos 2:9)**. Once again, Satan has failed to disrupt the seed-line from which God's Savior Jesus Christ would come.

Deductive Logic

The geological sciences of today have chronicled that monumental flooding did occur on earth during the time of Noah's flood. Episodes of mass destruction of an epic nature have been unearthed at the ancient biblical sites of Sodom and Gomorrah. Numerous other excavated cities of biblical antiquity have been unearthed including Bashan, a city built for housing giants. Anthropological sciences of today have discovered the remains of giant beings having lived on earth at one time. Early documents of history from different parts of the world of Mesopotamia and surrounding civilizations record ancient events of supernatural beings, the "great men of old," "giants," and horrific climatic events very similar to those of biblical scripture. The "Babylonian Creation Tablets," the Egyptian "Book of the Dead," and "the Assyrian Tablets" are such examples. Within the truths of these "mighty men of renown," long since forgotten over time, we may also have the origins of certain tales of the demigods and goddesses, which have evolved through the generations as written in Greek mythologies from these legends, memories, and traditions of man. From all of these sources, we find enough evidence of the fallen angles and their giant offspring inserted into the history of mankind that it is simply illogical not to give credence to such matters by anyone, including some Christians. There is much about the supernatural world of another dimension and supernatural beings that mankind does not know of or comprehend.

The Third Influx

Beginning in the book of **Matthew chapter 24** of the New Testament, the disciples asked of Jesus questions about the signs of His return (the second advent) and of the end times **(Matthew 24:3)**. The return of Jesus is also reported similarly in **Mark chapter 13 and Luke chapter 21**. In these individual accountings, Jesus explains the seven trumps (one through seven). The blow of a trumpet (trump) is representative of a sounding or call to action of the warnings of those things (prophesies) which must happen before His return as brought forth in **Revelation 8:7–14:1.**

The third influx of the fallen angels begins with the sounding of the sixth trump, ushering in Satan's return to earth as the antichrist with his angels. Satan's arrival occurs before the return (second advent) of our actual Lord and Savior Jesus Christ which will occur at the sounding seventh trump. The sixth trump begins with a war in heaven when the archangel Michael and his angels fight against Satan (AKA serpent, dragon, and devil) and his angels. Satan and his angels lose the battle and are then tossed out of heaven onto the earth by Michael and his angels **(Revelation 12:7–10)**. Heaven rejoices at Satan's removal from them but at the same time exclaim their sadness and grief for the inhabitants of earth **(Revelation 12:12)**.

In both **Luke 17:26–30 and Matthew 24:38**, Jesus warns us as He speaks to the disciples that in this end time when Satan and his fallen angels are cast down and return to earth, that it will be the same as in the days of Noah prior to the flood. Mankind will be rollicking on the earth in drinking, eating, taking of wives in marriage, days of great wickedness and ungodliness, wherein the Sons of God (Nephilim, fallen ones) were also taking women as their wives, any that they chose **(Genesis 6:1–5)**. For this reason, He also gives warning to women: "For this cause ought the woman to have power on her head because of the angels" **(1 Corinthians 11:10)**, the power (delegated authority) being that of Jesus Christ, that as a believer, no

STUDY 11

harm should come to her. And just as Noah's ark did save the last of those untouched by all the evilness when all else was destroyed, so will the Son of Man (Jesus Christ) return to save His followers **(Matthew 24:36–39)**. As believers in Christ, we do have power over Satan, his fallen angels, evil spirits, and all of our enemies—in His Name, in the name of Jesus Christ. Nothing, by any means shall hurt us **(Luke 10:17–20)**.

Satan and the fallen angels return to the earth to deceive as many as possible into worshiping him, having us believe that he is the Christ **(Matthew 24:23–24)**. We are not fighting a war against flesh man but of supernatural beings. Our weapons are not of man's creations but of God's; His armor for us is the only way we win. Our belt holds fast His truths. Our breastplate is righteousness, doing what is right in God's eyes, not man's. Our shoes store the knowledge of the good news of eventual, everlasting peace, and above all, our shield is that of faith, putting our trust in our heavenly Father. We have His promise of salvation and eternal life with Him through His Son Jesus Christ. We also have His sword, His Holy Spirit, which is the Word of God **(Ephesians 6:10–17)**.

Satan and his angels arrive peacefully, unexpectedly, in a time of careless security **(Daniel 11:21)**. Satan comes peacefully and prosperously **(Daniel 8:23–25)**. Most expect great violence to occur on earth at the time of his arrival; however, quite the opposite will happen as his role is that of the *anti*-christ. The word *anti* is Greek (#500/473), meaning "instead of." If he is to be successful with his lies and deceptions, he must act "as" Christ would, pretending to be loving, peaceful, caring, solving world problems, creating peace on earth, displaying supernatural abilities. In fact, his mode of operation will deceive the whole world **(Revelation 12:9)**. His array of supernatural feats and wonders, such as bringing lightning down from the sky, will only work to further convince the world to worship him, believing that he is Jesus Christ **(Revelation 13:13–18)**. He is not a man of flesh but a supernatural being, once a cherub angel, as are his followers all angelic spiritual beings from another dimension.

Angels were created by God and are His children. The fallen angels chose to follow Satan in his rebellion against our Father. They denied God and Jesus **(Jude 1:4)**. They left their place of habitation **(Jude 1:6)**. They refused to be born of the water of woman **(John 3:3–5)** even as Jesus was **(John 3:13)**. They violated God's law of nature in the subject of "kind after kind" **(1 Corinthians 15:38–39)**. Flesh is flesh, and spirit is spirit—two different varieties of creation **(John 3:6 8)**. These spiritual beings committed the sin of fornication with the daughters of flesh **(Genesis 6:2–5)**. This ungodly union resulted in a hybrid creation of their own—the Gibbors or Rapha which were not of God's creation. In like manner of Sodom and Gomorrah did they also sin going after "strange flesh," translated from the Greek as "heteros" (#2087), meaning other, of a different kind, the other of two. In other words, as the Sodomites (#6945), the Greek word meaning male prostitutes **(Jude 6–7)**.

Because of the ungodly wickedness committed by these fallen angels, God cast them down to the pit of darkness in chains awaiting their judgement **(2 Peter 2:4; Jude 6)**. Yet even with all of their sins against our Father, because of His love for all of His children and His fairness in absolute righteousness, He did offer His gift of forgiveness and eternal life to them the same as He does to all of us **(1 Timothy 2:4)**. For this reason, Jesus did go and preach God's message of salvation to them being held in prison, all the way back to the time of Noah **(1 Peter 3:19–20)**. However, as to the giants of old, the Gibbors or Rapha (deceased), they were the progeny of the union between spiritual beings and flesh beings and were not of God's creation, not His children, therefore He destroyed them all **(Isaiah 26:14)**.

Although this study is not given to the end time of this second earth age, we can clearly see this third influx of the fallen angels led by Satan himself as the antichrist does establish it. His and their period of tribulation brings nothing but troubles, suffering, pain, and misery for all of God's creations both in the heavens and on earth.

> **For in those days shall be affliction such as was not from the beginning of the creation which God created unto this time; neither shall be. (Mark 13:19)**

STUDY 11

And except that the Lord had shortened those days, no flesh should be saved; but for the elect's sake, whom He hath chosen, He hath shortened the days. (Mark 13:20)

As a believing Christian, we have no need to worry because through this all, we have our Father's promise: "But there shall not a hair of your head perish. In your patience possess ye your souls" **(Luke 21:18–19)**. After Satan's period of tribulation comes the return, the second advent of Jesus Christ ("Yahshua," meaning God the Savior) and the new heaven and the new earth and life eternal as put forward throughout God's Word **(The Bible)**. Have you read it?

If throughout all the deception and confusion brought about by Satan and his fallen angels on their return (at the sixth trump), and you have forgotten that the number six comes before the number seven, therefore you are not sure just who you might be about to worship, remember this: if you are still in your flesh body, it is Satan because at the instant of Jesus Christ return (at the seventh trump), *all* (the good, the bad, and the ugly) will be changed into our spiritual (angelic) bodies in "a twinkling of an eye" **(1 Corinthians 15:50–52)**.

Signs of the End

> Tell us, when shall these things be and what shall the signs be of Thy coming, and the end of the world?
> —Matthew 24:3

Introduction

The piercing blast of a trumpet can be heard great distances. The sound of a trumpet represents an alert and call to action. For centuries, the trumpet (trump) has sounded battle field commands of instruction, directives, and warnings against the enemy. It is with this same purpose and type of an alert that our heavenly Father has given us in advance (prophecy) within His written Word—His clear and loud warnings of who, what, where, and when certain events concerning the end of this earth age will transpire. With the end of this dispensation of time, it is instantly followed by the ushering in of God's new (rejuvenated) heaven and earth, cleansed of all evil and sin, perfectly restored exactly as decreed by our Father in accordance with His will **(Revelation 21:1–5)**.

The staging of these events in this age and their seasons are revealed to us in great detail from the book of **Revelation** (New Testament) of the Bible. These actions are principally separated into three headings—the "Seven Trumps," the "Seven Vials," and the "Seven Seals." As entitled, each heading has within itself seven different actions (numbered one through seven) of the events that will take place pertinent to each. In the most general sense, the subject of the seven seals is related to education **(Revelation chapters 6 and 8:1–6)**. The subject matter of the seven vials is related to God's wrath against His enemies **(Revelation chapter 16)**. The subject matter of the seven trumps is related to the actions or execution of God's commands which will occur both in heaven and on earth, culminating the end of this earth age and the instantaneous beginning of the new heaven and earth age with the second advent (return to earth) of Jesus Christ **(Revelation chapters 8 through 12)**.

Within a study of the book of **Revelation** (which this is not) we learn from the above information that the subject matter of the *sixth* trump, *sixth* vial, and *sixth* seal is in each instance of Satan (666).

> **Here is wisdom. Let him that hath understanding count the number of the beast; for it is the number of a man; and his number is Six hundred threescore, and six [666]. (Revelation 13:18)**

Through these numbered sequences of the trumps, vials, and seals, we are shown that the arrival on earth of Satan (the antichrist) and his period of tribulations (troubles) *comes before* the return of the true Jesus Christ, which isn't until the seventh seal, seventh vial, and seventh trump. The number six comes before the number seven.

End-time actions or events are found prophesized in the Old Testament of the Bible as well, such as in the book of **Zechariah chapter 14,** which in essence foretells some of the information given detail in the book of **Revelation**. In the book of **Daniel**, through his dream given by God, we find portrayed the destructive times (tribulation period) on earth surrounding the arrival of Satan preceding Christ's return. "For these are the days of vengeance that all things which are written may be fulfilled" **(Luke 21:22)**.

God gives us many warnings not to be deceived into believing that because he, Satan the antichrist, arrives first (before Jesus the true Christ) with his entourage of angelic beings demonstrating supernatural powers, pretending that he is Christ; he is not. Satan returns at the sixth trump whereas Jesus Christ does not return until the seventh trump.

BIBLE STUDIES 102

Purpose of this Study

The purpose of this Bible study is to illuminate Jesus's summary of events emerging in this generation, identifying the clues to the approaching end to this dispensation of time marking His return to earth (second advent). Jesus provides this information privately to His disciples in reply to their question: "Tell us, when shall these things be, and what shall be the signs of Thy coming, and of the end of the world" **(Matthew 24:3)**. At some time in our lives, most of us have given thought to this same question.

Since the time Jesus walked the earth over two thousand years ago, many unlearned persons have falsely proclaimed, "The end is nigh" with some going so far as to assign "dates and times" to their predictions based solely on man's speculations. People have tired of religions falsely claiming that Jesus's return will occur at any time (the "any moment" doctrine), which never seems to happen. We have been warned of such proclamations as prophesized (foretold) by our heavenly Father.

> **Knowing this first, that there shall come in the last days scoffers walking after their own lusts [desires], and saying Where is the promise of His coming? For since the fathers [prophets and apostles] fell asleep [died], all things continue as they were from the beginning of creation. (2 Peter 3:2–4)**

God instructs us for our own good that we must read His Word and be knowledgeable of the words spoken of by the holy prophets (Old Testament) and the apostles (New Testament). "Surely the Lord God will do nothing, but He revealeth His secret unto His servants the prophets" **(Amos 3:7)**.

The fact is, Jesus very plainly and directly states: "But of that day and hour [of the end time and His return] knoweth no man, no, not the angels of heaven; but My Father only" **(Matthew 24:36)**. Jesus does, however, provide us with a summary of warning signs (trumps) to the events which must occur first—those events that precede Satan's return as the antichrist, bringing with him times of great tribulation (troubles) on earth which, again to reiterate, takes place first *before* Jesus's return as King of kings and Lord of lords.

Jesus's response to His disciples concerning the signs preceding His return to earth and the final chapter of this world age are recorded in the New Testament books of **Matthew chapter 24, Mark chapter 13,** and **Luke chapter 21.** These three books of the four Gospels (good news of Jesus Christ) offer three individual narratives of Jesus's overview of the signs of the end times. Each is characterized by the simplicity in which Jesus teaches the "short version" in addressing the seven trumps, vials, and seals detailed in the book of **Revelation.**

Jesus's Summary of the Warning Signs

1. *The destruction of Jerusalem:* **(Matthew 24:1–2)**

Jesus declared: "See ye not all these things? Verily I say unto you; there shall not be left here one stone upon another that shall not be thrown down."

After speaking to the multitudes, Jesus and His disciples are walking through the city streets of Jerusalem and the disciples are in awe of the great buildings of stone and the temple. Jesus tells them that a time will come in the future when not one stone will be left upon another as the result of the utter destruction of those buildings.

Some today would have us believe that this occasion has already passed into history when the Roman general Titus attacked, destroyed, and pillaged Jerusalem in the year AD 70. However, we can clearly see that this assault by Titus was not the catastrophic event Jesus is prophesizing as evidenced by the existence of what is known today as "the wailing wall." The "wailing wall" is a portion of the old west city wall of Jerusalem which still remains standing to this day "stone upon stone." This great destruction of Jerusalem will not take place until Satan himself is sitting in the temple, being worshipped as God, showing himself to be God **(2 Thessalonians 2:1–5)** when at that instant of the seventh trump **(Revelation 11:15)**, Jesus's feet touch down on the earth at Mount Zion **(Revelation 14:1)**.

2. *False teaching:* **(Matthew 24:4)**

Jesus declared: "Take heed that no man deceive you." This is the leading warning that Jesus presents to us in His teaching of the signs of the last days—deception. Always verify a teaching given by any person alongside the truth of God's Word ensuring that you rightly divide His Word (a process detailed in another study) and prayerfully seek His guidance in discerning biblical truths regarding a statement, doctrine, tradition, or theology expounded by man.

One popular example of false teaching is the "rapture theory" (see "Rapture Theory Verses God's Word, the Bible" study). It was first expressed by a Ms. Margaret MacDonald in 1830, not God's Word. The word *rapture* is not in the Bible. God is against those teaching a "flyaway" doctrine to save their (His children) souls as stated in **Ezekiel 13:18–20**. With some 668 prophecies of the Bible having come to fruition to date, it isn't a bit unusual that our heavenly Father knew and forewarned us that the "rapture" doctrine would be created to cause confusion and deception by Satan for those of His children that didn't take the time or effort to read His letter He wrote to us, the Bible. This deception has even gone to the extent that some "Bibles" printed today have changed the above verse to something entirely different in meaning.

Christians and nonbelievers alike will be here on earth during Satan's period of tribulation. While here on earth during that time, Christians will continue with their service to God—to "plant seed" giving Christ's testimony **(1 Corinthians 3:6–9)**—and God's elect will stand before Satan, allowing the Holy Spirit to speak through them as a testimony before the whole earth **(Mark 13:9–11)**. Satan, the great deceiver, with his flood of lies "will deceive the whole world" **(Revelation 12:9)**. This very doctrine of man's (rapture theory) is likely to be one of Satan's biggest lies in deceiving many into worshiping him, the antichrist, believing he has come to "rapture" his followers from his tribulation period if only they will worship him.

STUDY 12

In conjunction with the "rapture theory," many are told that we don't have to read, to know, or understand the book of **Revelation** as we won't be here on earth during Satan's tribulation period anyway. The truth is, the book of **Revelation** (Greek word #602/601 *apokalupsis*, meaning disclosure, reveal, appearing, coming) or the revealing of Jesus Christ is His testimony given by God and is for the express purpose of showing His servants (Christians) things which must come to pass, ending this dispensation of time on earth to which He gives His personal blessing to those who do read and hear His prophecy **(Revelation 1:1–3)**.

3. *False teachers:* **(Matthew 24:5)**

Jesus declared: "For many will come in My name saying, I am Christ; and shall deceive many."

False teachings by supposed Christian (Christ-man) teachers of God's Word permeate many religions of the world today. In fact, despite mankind's historical evidence, not to mention biblical history, some believe that Jesus Christ has not yet come in the flesh. Of these teachers beware, for they are antichrists **(2 John 1:7)**. Many Christians are deceived and believe a lie because they are unaware of God's truths as they fail to read, study, and rightly divide God's Word for themselves. Instead, they have been relying on the word of man, his theologies, doctrines, and religious traditions rather than the Word of God for the truth. False teachers unrepentantly perpetuate untruths which deceive His children. For this reason, God's judgements begin at the very pulpits of His church **(1 Peter 4:17–18)**. And to those who would add to or take away from God's Word face being removed from God's Book of Life **(Revelation 22:19)**.

4. *Rumors of wars:* **(Matthew 24:6)**

Jesus declared: "And ye shall hear of wars and rumors of wars, see that ye be not troubled; for all these things must come to pass, but the end is not yet."

Threats of armed actions between nations and peoples terrorizing the world occur endlessly today—North Korea against the United States, Russia against Ukraine, Turkey against the Kurds, Iran against Egypt, Palestine against Israel, religion against religion, and many more. With all of this unrest in the world, Jesus tells us above not to be troubled. We need to remember that God is in control of all things, and we must maintain our faith in Him. His kingdom is coming, and His will is going to be carried out—in heaven and on earth. For His purpose, these things must come to pass as we march toward the everlasting era of the new heaven and earth.

5. *Wars:* **(Matthew 24:7)**

Jesus declared: "For nation shall rise against nation and kingdom against kingdom."

The increase of wars on earth during the last eighty years following World War I have surged exponentially since. We have seen World War II, Korean War, Vietnam War, Afghanistan/Russia, Falkland Islands, Afghanistan/United States, Lebanon, Iraq, Kuwait, Syria, several civil wars of African nations, and more. Most of the inhabitants of our world today is at odds with one another—nations against nations, kingdoms against kingdoms, peoples against peoples. Religious and political differences flare up into hatred and prejudices generating wars with greater intensity and frequency than ever before on earth.

6. *Famines and pestilences:* **(Matthew 24:7)**

Jesus declared: "There shall be famines and pestilences."

Food shortages and epidemics of disease plague the inhabitants of earth, taking the lives of millions even today amidst man's best scientific attempts to eradicate both afflictions one by one.

What appears to be a straightforward statement (famines and pestilences) requires a deeper explanation of its intended meaning which has been lost in translation from the Greek language of the New Testament into the English language. In the original Greek language, it is written: "Limoi kai limoi." This is a figure of speech called a "paronomasia."

A paronomasia is made up of rhyming words or the repetition of words similar in sound but may not necessarily make any sense standing on their own. As a figure of speech in common use, the people of a particular language would, however, be familiar with what is actually meant in its use. For example, a paronomasia in the English language might be "tit-for-tat," meaning one action creates or deserves another similar or equal action.

Limoi kai limoi, the words being defined individually are "limoi" (Greek word # 3042/3007), meaning scarcity, dearth, or famine and "kai" (Greek root word #3007) meaning to fail, be absent. From these defined meanings, we can begin to understand why the word *famine* had been chosen in translation as a more easily recognized description in place of "dearth" or "scarcity," but in doing so, it also loses the original intent as a paronomasia.

The English word *pestilences* is translated from the Greek word *loimos* (word #3061) meaning a plague. The English word *plague* has several definitions, most pertaining to "death" depending on its use including spiritual death, alienation of the soul from God, as originally intended here.

By properly remaining within the subject phrase of "signs of the end" while also maintaining a paronomasia type figure of speech, the more direct translation into English within the subject phrase is "dearths and deaths." The English word *dearths* means privation, scarcity, dear, want—such as in famine (as chosen in the original translation)—and "death," as used in the spiritual sense (a spiritual death), is an alienation of the soul from God.

To further reinforce the subject phrase of "signs of the end time," our heavenly Father defined "famine in the last days" not as famine for food or water but rather for the Word of God **(Amos 8:11–12)**.

With this in-depth translation of "famine and pestilence" as translated in the Gospels, we are able to better understand its intended meaning as a scarcity or privation of the whole truths of the Word of God resulting in the spiritual deaths of many—"dearth and death." We only need to step inside most churches of the world to recognize this present-day reality; the Bible just isn't taught "precept upon precept, line upon line that man might be made to understand His doctrine," God's Word (paraphrased from **Isaiah 28:9–10**).

7. *Earthquakes:* (**Matthew 24:7**)

Jesus declared: "And earthquakes in divers [different] places."
Government records indicate both the frequency and strength of earthquakes have increased more during the last ten-year period than the entire preceding fifty years. Thousands of lives are lost each year as a result of these cataclysmic events and their aftermaths. An example of a "divers" location is Mineral, Virginia, ninety miles from Washington, DC on August 23, 2011. This was the strongest earthquake (5.8 magnitude) east of the Mississippi River since 1944. Earthquakes have been occurring more frequently on ocean floors too, sending resulting tidal waves of water (tsunamis) halfway around the world, devastating every shore in their path—Solomon Islands (2010), West Java Indonesia (2006), Indian Ocean (2004), and others.

8. *Just the beginning:* (**Matthew 24:8**)

Jesus declared: "All these things are only the beginning of sorrows."
The word *sorrows* as used here is translated from the Greek word *odin* (#5604/3601) meaning pang, as in birth or labor pain, travail, grief, or sorrow.

Summarizing Jesus's Declarations So Far

Through His warning signs so far, Jesus has shown us that the mass deception of the world by Satan's flood of lies (**Revelation 12:9**) has begun, generated very subtly today through the false teachings of false teachers. The lack (dearth) of God's truths to be taught as established in God's Word is the reason for the spiritual deaths of countless souls and their possible eternal alienation from God.

Constant warring between nations and rumors of war, the absence of peace, is causing worldwide deaths, unrest, agony, and worrisome tormenting grief for everyone as day-to-day stress becomes a part of living without faith in our heavenly Father. The earth itself has begun to experience birthing/labor pangs such as earthquakes causing other environmental impacts far beyond a supposed "earth warming," as never before seen in its history.

All of this is just the beginning of troubles preparing the way for Satan's appearance on earth and his attempt to deceive the world as the antichrist (pretending to be Jesus Christ), a supernatural being with supernatural powers who will claim he has come to "save the world," bringing world "peace and prosperity" **(Daniel 8:24–25)** with the greatest deceptions ever imagined. It is no wonder the whole world will worship him instead of the true Christ, thinking he is Christ, ignorant of the truth.

A Few Additional Signs of the "Latter Days"

God provides many other warning signs placed throughout the entire Bible. We need to be paying attention to them as they become life's realities in these latter days, exactly as prophesized some two thousand seven hundred years ago, seven hundred years before the birth of Jesus, some earlier yet and many more recent as we realize this age is drawing to a close. We have to read the Bible to stay in tune with His news. "But take ye heed; behold, I have foretold you all things" **(Mark 13:23)**. God keeps no secrets, and He tells it just as it is. Being oblivious to His truths or personally offended by them is not His fault or problem but ours alone. A child of God (Christian/Christ-man) is a reality, not a religion.

Isaiah 3:4–5, 9, paraphrased as follows:

Government leaders will be as children, ruling as immature babes, without wisdom **(v. 4)**.

People shall be oppressed (Hebrew #5065, meaning taxed, distressed, tyrannized) and children shall behave proudly (Hebrew #7092, meaning to embolden, act insolently) against the ancient

(Hebrew #2204, meaning aged) and base (Hebrew # 7034, meaning to hold in contempt and despise) the honorable **(v. 5)**.

Homosexuality will be brought out into the open, the sin of their actions declared (Hebrew #6440/6435, meaning countenance), no longer hidden, just as in the times of Sodom and Gomorrah **(v. 9)**.

1 Timothy 4:1–3, paraphrased as follows:

Some will leave the faith, seducing spirits and doctrines of the devil (devil worship) without any conscience **(vv. 1–2)**.

The institution of marriage is abandoned by many and some will abstain from meats which God created to be eaten by mankind **(v. 3)**.

2 Timothy 3:1–4, paraphrased as follows:

"This know also, that in the last days perilous times shall come" **(v. 1)**.

Mankind will become lovers of themselves (selfish), lovers of money (covetous), boasters (braggarts), present an air of being better than others (proud), hurtful and slanderous against others and against God (blasphemers), disobedient to parents, insubordinate, rebellious, and unholy (wicked) **(v. 2)**.

Mankind will become hard-hearted, void of a natural affection toward one another, breaking promises, lying against others, lack self-control, and savagely despise those who do good **(v. 3)**.

Mankind will be quick to betray others, a traitorous impulse, heady or rash behavior, high-minded, lovers of pleasures more than lovers of God **(v. 4)**.

2 Timothy 4:4, paraphrased as follows:

Man will substitute fables (myths) for God's truths. Christmas has become a time of shopping for gifts, parties, Santa Clause, and projections of massive retail sales in hopes of profitable gains rather than the conception of our Lord and Savior, Jesus Christ—the truth of God's doctrine (see "The Birth of Jesus Christ" study). Easter has turned into a ritual of spring time renewing, student vacations, new clothes, flowers, candy, hunting for decorated eggs, the Easter Bunny, and religious traditions rather than the resurrection of our Lord and Savior, Jesus Christ, His death the price for our sins, and His becoming our Passover **(1 Corinthians 5:7–8)**—the truth of God's doctrine **(v. 4)**.

STUDY 12

Notable Statistics of Resulting Factors of Some of These "Signs"

Juvenile delinquency first became nationally recognized as a growing problem in the United States around 1944 by the efforts of Ms. Emma Puschner, a White House consultant for what became the federal Aid to Families with Dependent Children program. The magnitude of the absence of the family structure and family values present today bears little if any resemblance to any other generation at any time in the past. This lack of rudimentary human behavior toward one another continues to nurture a growing lawlessness within generations of adults on earth today exactly as foretold.

The global war of terror against Christianity, Christian nations, and other religions is intensifying dramatically. Radical Islam claims it is the exalted religion of the world, and nothing is exalted above it. Their acts of terrorisms began being recorded in 1979 with one. During the decade of the '80s, there were five incidents, in the '90s, there were eight, from 2000 to 2010, there were nineteen, and between 2010 through March of 2019, there have been two hundred forty-four acts of terrorism claimed by these groups of Islamic religious radicals.

Our study of the Bible has taught us that life begins at conception (see "The Birth of Jesus Christ" study). Since the decriminalization of abortions in the United States in 1973, it is estimated there have been approximately fifty-four million children aborted (their lives terminated) in the United States alone. Worldwide, it is estimated that fourteen million abortions take place each year. Recently some states have passed legislation that allows the abortion terminology to include full-term births to be terminated as well.

The Apostasy

With all of these signs presented, and there are more, they culminate in the most evident sign to transpire today making way for the return of Satan prior to the second advent of Jesus Christ, that which is termed "the great apostasy."

Apostasy comes from the Greek word *apostosia*, meaning; defection, revolt from, abandonment or falling away from what one believed in; as apostasy from religion.

The Bible makes it very clear in the book of **2 Thessalonians 2:3:**

> **Let no man deceive you by any means; for that day [Christ's return] shall not come except there come a falling away [apostasy] first and that man of sin be revealed, the son of perdition [Satan].**

People certainly don't want to hear or talk about God, His Son Jesus, or the Holy Spirit today. Their reactions go anywhere from embarrassment to rage. "Religion" is one of two subject matters of which we are warned not to speak about publicly as it may "offend" someone, and at the very least, the wrongdoer faces severe "chastisement" if the "rule" is violated. It just simply isn't the "politically correct" thing to do in this age.

With Jesus's declarations regarding His warning signs of "deception" and "dearth and death" as a beginning to this apostatizing movement, it isn't hard to see that these signs clearly signal the paving of the way for Satan's supernatural arrival. They open wide the door for his deceiving the whole world, particularly when combined with his prophesized show of miracles.

> **And he doeth great wonders, so that he maketh fire come down from heaven on the earth in the sight of men. And deceiveth them that dwell on the earth by the means of those miracles. (Revelation 13:13–14)**

> **And all that dwell upon the earth shall worship him whose names are not written in the book of life of the Lamb slain from the foundation of the world. (Revelation 13:8)**

STUDY 12

When?

The question still remains: when? We see all of these signs today! Again to repeat what was stated earlier, no one knows—not man, not the angels in heaven, not even Jesus—only our Father **(Mark 13:32)**.

Jesus very emphatically tells us: "Now learn a parable of the fig tree; when her branch is yet tender and putteth forth leaves [not fruit], ye know that summer is near" **(Mark 13:28)**.

The parable of the fig tree is found in **Jeremiah chapter 24.** This is the prophecy (now a reality) of Israel once again becoming a nation. Israel hasn't existed as a nation for almost 2,500 years until the year 1948 (see "The Parable of the Fig Tree" study). This historic event is the prophetic sign of the latter days establishing the beginning point of the last generation of the end time.

Again, very emphatically, Jesus tells us: "Verily I say unto you that this generation shall not pass till all these things be done" **(Mark 13:30)**. A generation by biblical definitions has three possibilities—forty years **(Numbers 14:28–35)**, seventy years **(Psalms 90:10)**, and a hundred twenty years **(Genesis 6:3)**. Since the year 1948, we can see that the forty- and seventy-year definitions of "generation" are behind us now, leaving the one hundred twenty definition remaining.

"So in like manner, when ye see these things [signs] come to pass, know that it is nigh, even at the door" **(Mark 13:29)**.

Jesus tells us that life on earth during these last days will be just like it was during the days before the flood of Noah's time. "For as the days before the flood, they were eating and drinking, marrying and giving in marriage, until the day that Noah enter into the ark" **(Matthew 24:38)**. The world is oblivious to these times as the daily routines of life continue around the earth with no—or little—attention given to God's warnings stated over and over again as to just how things will be and what to look for in identifying the signs of the end times today, just as He did in Noah's time before the earth's destruction by flood waters in that day. Those that did not listen at that time were destroyed as will those who refuse to listen and heed the warnings of our Father today by worshiping the antichrist.

Jesus gives warning: "Take ye heed, watch and pray; for ye know not when the time is" **(Mark 13:33)**.

Jesus reiterates: "And what I say unto you I say unto all—**watch!**" **(Mark 13:37)**

In all of these things, remember Jesus tells us (Christian believers) not to be troubled by them. To be sure that we understand His message, He tells us again very clearly:

> **And ye shall be hated of all men for My name's sake. But there shall not an hair of your head perish. (Luke 21:17–18)**
>
> **In your patience possess ye your souls. (Luke 21:19)**
>
> **Watch ye therefore, and pray always that ye may be accounted worthy to escape all these things that shall come to pass, and to stand before the Son of Man. (Luke 21:36)**

Shadrach, Meshach, and Abed-nego of the Old Testament are our examples of faith in God, who when refusing to worship another god, were thrown into a furnace seven times hotter than required yet walked out without one hair on their heads being singed **(Daniel chapter 3)**.

One last thought for us all to remember is if on Satan's arrival on earth we are not quite sure as to what is happening because of his great powers of deception, pinch yourself. If you are still in a flesh body, you can be assured it is Satan and not Jesus Christ. Do not worship him. At the sounding of the seventh (the last) trump when Jesus truly returns, we are all (the good, the bad, and the ugly) instantly changed into our spiritual bodies **(1 Corinthians 15:51–52)**. Another piece of good news is Jesus tells us that Satan's ability to deceive the world is so great "[a]nd except those days should be shortened, there should no flesh be saved; but for the elect's sake those days shall be shortened" **(Matthew 24:22)**. He shortened Satan's period of tribulation

STUDY 12

from seven years **(Daniel 9:27)** to five months **(Revelation 9:5)** with a deeper explanation of these "times" brought forth in a future study.

Love, praise, and give thanks always to our heavenly Father for His love, blessings, and His gift of eternal life freely given to all those who, with repentant hearts, believe in His Son, Jesus Christ **(John 3:16)**.

About the Author

The author devotes his labors to serving God following his retirement from federal service in 2010. He and his wife live in the serenity of Michigan's Upper Peninsula where he works researching Bible scriptures that others may gain understanding through simplified home studies. They are blessed with five children, fourteen grandchildren, one great-grandchild, and their cat.